Content

Story Name

Fan boy's Email[1]

I never met Steve Jobs in person, but I have a story that is worth telling.

Stewart Brand is a friend of mine. He was also friends with Steve Jobs. Once I was visiting with Stewart and he said "Would you like to meet Steve Jobs?" And of course I said, "Sure!" I assumed he meant that he would invite us both to dinner or something like that on some future visit of mine to Silicon Valley.

But a few days later I got an email from Steve Jobs that said "How can I help you?" I got the idea that he thought I was asking for a meeting with him for some business purpose. But I didn't have anything like that.

So all I could think to do was pretty lame. I wrote him a lovely little fan boy email saying how much I admire him, etc. **He never answered**.

Morning workout with Steve Jobs[2]

I never did speak to Steve Jobs directly, but I saw him every morning for an entire summer at the Equinox gym in Palo Alto. He was in there around 5:20AM, wearing black pants and a black shirt, and seemed to do exactly the same workout every day.

30 min brisk walk, at a good incline.

I'd usually do a morning spin class, or just spin training by myself across the room from him. The way the treadmills and bikes were set up - we'd end up looking right at each other if I looked left. We locked eyes for quite a while, and occasionally did the "hello" nod every once in a while. As cheesy as it may be, I found it incredibly motivating to **"work out with Steve Jobs" every morning.**

I never did quite build up the courage to approach him and talk to him, however. It didn't seem right, and I didn't want to kick off his day on a bad note. (Being accosted by some selfish start up kid trying to make his way in the valley).

My girlfriend at the time did manage to get a chuckle out of Steve one day. She went for a light jog on the treadmill next to him. She was a tad bit clutzy while running (who isn't), and accidentally unplugged her headphones at one point, causing her running app to spew some statistics about her run very loudly. She almost tripped trying to silence the iPhone, and Steve seemed to find the entire event pretty amusing.

House Trip[3]

Steve Jobs attended Reed College starting in fall 1972. While he attended the college formally for only a semester, he spent an extra 18 months dropping in classes and crashing in his friends' rooms or in the couches in the school's Student Union building. The following is an experience recounted by some Reed College students, who showed up at his residence after about 25 years of Jobs' leaving the college.

In the winter of 1996–97, a band of Reedies including Justin Campbell '99 and Colin McCluney '99 took the Doyle Owl on a road trip to California. On a whim, **they stopped by Steve's house in Palo Alto and rang the bell.** They were floored when Steve emerged, admired the Owl, talked about Reed, and posed for this photo in Justin's parents' minivan. "He was really nice about it," Justin says.

Client Gift[4]

In about 1992 I was working at Chikwenya Camp in Mana Pools National Park, Zimbabwe.

This is a World Heritage Site, stunningly beautiful and, especially in those days, very isolated.

The maximum number of visitors was 12 and they slept in basic but comfortable tents. The dining area was an awning strung up between some trees overlooking the Zambezi River. We used old series 2 Land Rovers for game drives. On the river a platform tied over four canoes with a small motor was used. Walking safaris were very popular. Everyone who worked there was passionate about wildlife.

One day, during the siesta time in the heat of the day, getting ready for the next safari, I noticed a fellow guide, Clive, playing with a strange Rubik's cube-type puzzle.

I asked him, "What's that"?

"A puzzle thing", he answered. **"One of the clients gave it to me".**

"Which one" I asked.

"Steve", he said.

"Cool", I said, "He seems like quite a good bugger."

"Uhuh", said Clive, "he invented the Apple".

"What the ****'s the Apple?" I asked.

"Some sort of computer", said Clive.

"Oh", I said.

At the time, he was just another visitor. We liked him because he appreciated the beautiful place and was fascinated by the wildlife. At mealtimes (which were shared at one table) we all enjoyed the conversations with him.

When I eventually learned to turn on and much later use a computer, I discovered who he was and what he had done.

Good bugger too.

Steve Jobs lunch with Eric Schmidt[5]

At Palo Alto High School, we are allowed to go off campus for our break periods. We conveniently have Town & Country right across the street with many cafes and places to get a bite (expensive, though!).

On March 26th, 2010 my English class was let out early for lunch (I believe there was a rally that day, though not sure), and being the freshman that I was, I promptly headed for T&C to grab a smoothie or pizza slice. When I walked across the parking lot, I noticed that there was a Mercedes parked somewhat awkwardly (or it seemed kinda awkward to me) in front of Calafia's. When I got in front of Calafia's, **I saw Steve Jobs with another man sitting at a tiny table with lunch already finished.** I couldn't really believe it at first, and I walked past them again. I then walked past a few friends and Spencer Schoeben, and they asked me if Steve Jobs was still there. It was very surreal, seeing someone who created Apple sitting, having a chat right across the street from your high school. I later learned that the other guy sitting with him was Eric Schmidt, then **chief executive of Google**.

Water on Cigarette[6]

About '82 or '83, I and 5 others, including Steve, had dinner together in NYC. The now legendary, late Jay Chiat, then CEO of Chiat-Day Advertising, invited his client Steve, and his other client, Pioneer Electronics CEO Jack Doyle and his wife Ann, Pioneer's ad manager, and me, Pioneer Senior VP Marketing and Product Development, to dinner.

Dinner was over and while we waited for dessert, Ann lit up a cigarette (remember this was the early '80's in NYC), holding it away and blowing smoke away from the rest of us at the table. Steve, who was seated next to Ann, gave no indication that this bothered him. He simply went on talking animatedly as he had all dinner.

At one point Ann put her lit cigarette in an ashtray the opposite side of Steve. He never looked at it but must have seen her put it down because without so much as a glance toward her or the cigarette, without breaking from whatever topic he was currently holding forth on **at that moment, he reached across her, picked the cigarette up from the ashtray, and dropped it in her half full water glass.**

I can still see the stunned looks on everyone's face except Steve who continued to educate the rest of us on . . . I have no idea.

No doubt Steve was a genius given all he and Apple, under his direction, later accomplished. However based on what I've heard about him personally, and witnessed that night, he's not a person I would care to spend time with. One dinner was more than enough.

Recruiter of Sun Microsystems[7]

In 1988, I was self-employed as a recruiter and had referred a number of candidates to Steve at NeXT Computer, which he subsequently hired. I had also worked at Sun Microsystems as a contract recruiter. In September of that year, Steve invited me to his offices on Deer Creek Road in Palo Alto for an informal interview. He was 45 minutes late. As soon as Steve led me into his office and closed the door, he turned and said, **"You recruited for Sun and Sun hires shitty people."**

"Well," I retorted, "You hired the ones Sun didn't want."

At that point, **Steve cracked a big smile and exclaimed, "Touché!"**

After that, we had a nice chat for about twenty minutes. During this time, a crowd of NeXT employees gathered and placed outside. When Steve opened the door to escort me out, he was mobbed like a celebrity, while I was shoved aside. As I was about to exit the lobby, I heard Steve call out my name. I turned and saw Steve bending down and waving to me, childlike. I walked away thinking to myself, "That guy can be a real jerk, but he sure is charming."

Long Sleeve[8]

One day in Fall 2010, not long after starting a full-time job at Apple, my friend Lita visited me at 1 Infinite Loop. It was a nice, warm, sunny day. We were getting lunch at Cafe Macs, waiting in line for some salmon teriyaki. When I turned around in line, I was surprised to find Steve Jobs right behind us. What's most interesting was that he wasn't wearing his usual black turtleneck sweater. Instead, he had on this black-and-white-striped long-sleeved shirt, which I'd never seen him wear before. Lita whispered to me, "OMG that's Steve Jobs!"

After we had our lunch, we decided to get some gelato. Cafe Macs served _amazing_ gelato. Incredibly, Steve was right behind us again! My friend couldn't hold it in any longer and said something random like "Isn't it a bit warm to be wearing that shirt?" **Steve replied, "But I don't have any short sleeve shirts!"** And that was that. It was totally random, but very amusing.

Elevator Buttons[9]

A friend of mine once found themselves alone in an elevator with Steve Jobs. My friend was excited, and wanted to say something to him. However, Jobs looked totally preoccupied and was staring ahead with tremendous intensity, squinting his eyes.

My friend didn't know what was going on, and got really uncomfortable. Finally, Jobs snapped out of his trance and asked my friend, **"What do you think of these elevator buttons?"**

My friend was totally confused and didn't know what to say. My friend is not shy and generally has an opinion on most things. However, he thought nothing about the font or colour of the elevator buttons, and was rendered totally speechless.

Vic Gundotra, Google SVP, posted a similar account of Jobs preoccupation with design that most people miss. Gundotra was working with Jobs on the first iPhone and the NY Times wrote about the experience:

Mr Gundotra said Mr Jobs had called him on a Sunday morning with an "urgent issue, one that I need addressed right away." Mr Jobs said: "I've been looking at the Google logo on the iPhone and I'm not happy with the icon. The second O in Google doesn't have the right yellow gradient. It's just wrong and I'm going to have Greg fix it tomorrow. Is that O.K. with you?"

The hundreds of designers who had been involved in the iPhone development didn't notice that the shading in a yellow O might have a slightly incorrect gradient. But Mr Jobs did.

Marital Dispute[10]

We were having family pictures taken at the Gamble Garden in Palo Alto, a few blocks from Steve's house, in 2011. Our young daughters were dressed adorably for the pictures, and we had our very charismatic Vizsla / Weimaraner dog, Mocha, with us.

We spotted Steve sitting on a park bench casually chatting with a friend.

We approached Steve and asked if he could settle a marital dispute for us. Without any hint of a smile he responded **"if I can have one of your children".** We offered the dog, then my wife told the story of the naming contest. Steve said that Apple had a large marketing department to do things like pick names for their computers, and it was absurd to think they'd leave that to fifth graders. My wife was crestfallen; we thanked him for his time and excused ourselves, at which point he and his friend left the garden. With regards to his demeanour, I would say he "suffered" our inquiry, which is to say there was no indication of interest on his behalf in participating in this conversation, although I do appreciate the implied compliment regarding our daughters.

As a postscript, my wife contacted her fifth-grade teacher, who recounted the whole story of the contest in astonishing detail. It turns out an education software company had been running a pilot project in the classroom using Apple computers, and indeed did have a contest to name the computer, though Apple had nothing to do with this. Once we did the math we also figured out this was five years before the Mac was launched, so it was more likely centred on the Apple II+.

Good companies make mistakes[11]

In 1999 Apple flubbed orders of a release of PowerMac computers because Motorola couldn't deliver the 500 MHz CPUs. Apple summarily cancelled the orders that were in the system and there was something of an outcry over this. I contacted the regional Apple sales rep, a very nice lady who said to me, "I agree with everything you're complaining about, and all I can tell you is sj@pixar.com." At the time, this was an email address that Steve used personally. I sent this email:

"When you're right, you're really right, and when you're wrong, you are SPECTACULARLY wrong. This is one of the later cases. Fix this problem, admit the mistake, take the lumps financially and preserve your customer base.

I suggest: Ship all orders as promised, except for the 500 MHz boxes. Ship those with 450 chips and a rebate, or offer to fill the orders when chips are available.

Oh, and just one more thing: APOLOGIZE!!"

He wrote back

"We decided to do exactly this last evening, and are communicating this to those who placed orders on the Apple Store.

Thanks
Steve"

But, the interesting part is that I wrote back to him say, among other things, "good companies make mistakes, great companies fix them" and that was in the Apple press release!

CUPERTINO, CALIFORNIA - October 18, 1999 - "We aim to delight our customers, and we clearly dropped the ball in this instance. We apologize to our customers for upsetting and disappointing them during this past week," said Steve Jobs, Apple's interim CEO. "Our actions today will hopefully set things right. As the old business proverb says: **Good companies make mistakes. Great companies fix them.**"

I totally made it up. I've never heard that phrase before or since. Glad SJ liked it.

Father-Daughter Dance[12]

We live sort of near Steve. He used to drive by on his way to work and always blew right through the corner stop sign. No plates on his car either. I sometimes thought "what an arrogant prick." But I also thought, "Maybe he shouldn't have to stop, as he's probably on his way to do great things today."

We'd go to his house on Halloween. It was always done up very well and they would be outside in costume, giving out something healthy/nasty like Odwalla bars. One time he was there, in all black, stirring a large, steaming cauldron. I told my daughter to say "Dude, you're getting a Dell" but she chickened out. Instead, she asked him what was in the pot. He replied, "Children."

The last time I saw him was at a school **"father-daughter" dance**. He looked so frail and small you just knew he was going to die. It made me feel guilty. Here was this man with so much to contribute, dying, while I, a schlepped, am fine.

Apple cafeteria[13]

Back in 2009, right around the Snow Leopard launch, and less than a month prior to my birthday, I shipped out from Vancouver, BC to beautiful Cupertino for my two weeks of training to be an Apple Genius.

During my stay, I ate around California where I could, but **mainly I just grabbed my meals from the Apple cafeteria, Café Macs.** The food was great anyway, and the place was always bustling with all sorts of characters, one of which during my stay was Johnny Knoxville.

So this goes on a while until the day before Snow Leopard launches. I'm in line with a few other trainee colleagues to get my food, and Steve Jobs gets in behind is. The chatty one of the group doesn't waste any time, and asks "Have you got a favourite dish?" He replies with a soft smile "The burritos are actually really good." (Indeed they are!) The chatter goes on a little longer, mostly about us being new faces, what we do at Apple, if we like it so far, etc. I still can't decide what it was about him, but he had this way of making you feel like you were the only one in the world that mattered when you talked to him. He set the bar high from that day forward in my interactions with others. After we parted ways, he went off with his food, joining Jonathan Ive in the corner. No doubt discussing whatever amazing ideas they had, smiling as they did.

The next day, Snow Leopard launched, with a raucous gathering at the Apple campus, and drinks for all. It was an incredible gathering of intelligent, talented, and cheerful people. Not even I could wipe off the stupid smirk when we received our swag.

Non-Descript Building[14]

I'd met Jobs on several occasions but never spoke more than a hello to him.

But one year, after a Macworld Expo, a friend and I were walking down the street and I saw him and his wife standing on the street corner, just looking around. **It seemed kind of odd that they were just standing there, looking across the street and pointing to a non-descript building.** I walked up to him and congratulated him on yet another great keynote he had given at the expo. He asked me how I liked the new products and if I planned on buying them.

I laughed and handed him a business card and began to explain what I did. He looked at it, interrupted me and said, "Oh, I know you..."

Oh shit...

I stammered a lame "thank you..." (I don't think he meant it that way - I've been in hot water with Apple PR a few times over the years), congratulated him again and walked away.

It wasn't until years later I realized why he was standing where he was. We were in New York City and it was on 5th Ave...Right across the street from where the 5th Avenue Apple store would be eventually built. He was "scouting" the location. :)

Steve Jobs Greatest Creations[15]

My daughter was 5, so it must have been 11 years ago, when we went to the Kona Village Resort in Hawaii. It is an all-inclusive family resort with lots of free standing cabanas and some larger villa type accommodations, and a general dining area. One day I realized that the guy having lunch, in shorts and a tee-shirt, sitting a table or two over from me, was Steve Jobs.

After lunch he continued to sit at the table surrounded by a small group who listened as he talked. As I recall, at least one was actually sitting on the deck at his feet. I figured he was there with his family and didn't really want to have people bugging him, so I didn't go over, and what would I have said anyway, **"HI, I have a mac and I love your products?"**

A couple of days later, I signed up to go on a glass bottom boat tour. My wife, my daughter and I boarded the boat, and after a few minutes, Steve and his wife and their kids got on and we pulled away from the dock, just our two families. I still didn't want to bug him, but at some point as I stood next to him and we both watched our fascinated kids peering into the depths through the clear green water, I said, **"They are just amazing aren't they?" To which he responded quietly, "My greatest creations."**

Hung up on Steve Jobs[16]

In 2006, my friend was working as an assistant to a very high profile agent at one of the big talent agencies in Los Angeles. His role as "gatekeeper" on the phone was perhaps the most valuable. Imagine how many aspiring actors, writers, and other assorted charlatans would try to get his boss's ear on a daily basis. It was my friend's job to deflect the BS calls and make sure only those with important business matters to discuss would get through.

One day, the phone rings and the voice on the other line says **"Hi. This is Steve Jobs calling for [agent]."**

My friend: "Yeah right, pal. **Good try." And hangs up.**

The phone rings again.

Voice: **"Hi. It's really Steve.** Can I please talk to [agent]? I have an important matter to discuss."

My friend: "Seriously, dude. Don't call back again."

Third time.

Voice: "Hi. I know you don't believe me, but hang up, look at your Caller ID, and you'll see that it's from Apple. Call that number back and ask my assistant for me."

And he hangs up.

My friend looks up the number and, sure enough, it was a line at Apple. He calls the number back, Steve's assistant answers and says "This happens a lot. He'll be right on."

Reason :

My friend's boss ran talent division, and Justin Long was one of the agency's clients. The first batch of Mac vs. PC ads, starring Long and John Hodgman, were wildly successful, and Apple wanted to shoot another batch. At the time, Justin was working on a film, so he or his agent had told the creative working on the campaign that he was unavailable to shoot more. Steve was calling to ask if there was anything my friend's boss could do.

Apple Intern[17]

I met Steve Jobs randomly while working as an intern at Apple in the summer of 2010. I had stepped into an elevator on the main Apple campus when, just as the door was closing, Steve Jobs strolled in. **He saw that I had an intern badge on, and asked me what I was working on over the summer.**

When he asked me this question, I wasn't sure what to say. Should I tell him what I was working on, and risk getting in trouble for disclosing what I was working on (as we had been instructed not to do during orientation), or should I just tell him that I wasn't allowed to tell him?

I went with the latter, telling him, "Sorry, but I'm not supposed to tell you." Steve flashed a smile, chuckled a little, and stepped out of the elevator.

Steve Jobs ID[18]

Not exactly MEETING him, but...

When I was at the University of Pennsylvania in 1989, some sales folks from NeXT did a demo of the NeXT Cube to some students at the Distributed Systems Lab. I noted on their business cards that NeXT email addresses were of the form firtname_lastname@next.com. On a lark, I shot off a note to Steve_Jobs@next.com asking if he read his own email and expressing my fan boy sentiments.

I received the following reply:
From Steve_Jobs@NeXT.COM Fri Jan 27 00:40:55 1989
Posted-Date: Thu, 26 Jan 89 21:41:51 PST
Received-Date: Fri, 27 Jan 89 00:40:50 EST
Received: from next.NeXT.COM by sunset.NeXT.COM (4.0/NeXT0.0-Aleph)
 id AA11546; Thu, 26 Jan 89 21:41:03 PST
Message-Id: <8901270541.AA11546@sunset.NeXT.COM>
Received: from renaissance.NeXT.COM (renaissance.NeXT.COM.18.129.IN-ADDR.ARPA) by next.NeXT.COM (4.0/SMI-4.0Beta)
 id AA01566; Thu, 26 Jan 89 21:46:27 PST
Received: by renaissance.NeXT.COM (NeXT-0.8/SMI-4.0Beta)
 id AA01780; Thu, 26 Jan 89 21:41:51 PST
Date: Thu, 26 Jan 89 21:41:51 PST
From: Steve_Jobs@NeXT.COM
To: remaker@eniac.seas.upenn.edu
Subject: re: Just a hunch....
Status: R

Phil.

Yes, I do have an Internet address. Please help me by not spreading this fact around indiscriminately....

Thanks for the feedback.
I'm glad you like our little machine.

Take care,
Steve Jobs.

Steve Jobs - Sampling Sony[19]

I was in the Sony Style store at the Stanford Mall. I can't remember what it was I was buying.

As I was waiting in the checkout line, I realized that Steve was 2 people ahead of me. He was wearing his usual black turtleneck and faded blue jeans. **He was holding a projector.**

"So I'd like to get this repaired," he said to the obviously bored cashier.

To my surprise, the man at the counter seemed totally oblivious to his identity.

"Okay," he responded, "What name do you want it under for pickup?"

"Just put it under Steve," he said.

Steve then walked over to the laptop section, and started sampling some of the VAIOs on display.

I was completely flabbergasted, and after several minutes, worked up the courage to walk on over to Steve. I was barely able to utter a, "Hello...Mr Jobs."

Steve Jobs looked over at me, gave me his biggest smile, and responded with a friendly "hello!"

He went back to looking at the competition, as I left, but I will always remember the time I met the one, the only Steve Jobs.

Girl Interested in Me[20]

This was in June '10 just a few days before Apple's WWDC. I was working late out of a cafe and was testing one of my apps on the iPad. This was in India and at that time the iPad hadn't been officially launched here, so was something that would definitely catch someone's eye.

There was this girl sitting on the next table and was pretty curious about this new thing, moments later she stopped by and we had a nice chat about how cool the iPad is, and was pretty impressed that I could actually write an app that could run on it.

I went home and before going to bed wrote a short email to Steve about how an iPad got a girl interested in me and almost forgot about it until.... Days later, it was his WWDC keynote and I was following a few live blogs that night as I always do (I was GMT +5:30), then suddenly I saw something that was very familiar, it was my email that Steve displayed on the huge screen behind him. He said **"It is magical, I know it because I got this email: I was sitting in a café with my iPad, and it got a girl interested in me!"**

This is something I'd cherish for the rest of my life :)

Navigated to Steve Jobs house[21]

I never met Steve Jobs, but did have kind of a poignant moment. One of my first jobs out of school was working for Macworld Magazine, so I had been a long time Steve fan and had followed his travails for some time - I was in the unenviable position of constantly defending the Mac to roommates who were die hard PC guys well into the 90s.

Fast forward 15 years. About 1 week after his passing I was driving down the Embarcadero Road in Palo Alto going to see a client, and I was 20 minutes early. This odd compulsion to drive by his house and see it first-hand took over, and I pulled out my iPhone and pretty quickly found out I was about 3 blocks away. I thought it was weird - what exactly was I planning to do? Either way, I made my decision, took a quick right and navigated to the spot where his house was.

I slowed down, took a look, and was taken by how nice yet humble it was - beautiful gardens, beautiful home, not surrounded by big gates or security - you could have just walked right up to the front door. I kind of snapped out of it and thought **"Ok, turn around and going, this is pretty weird." Right where I was spinning a U-turn I stopped and saw the infamous silver Mercedes, just parked right out front around the corner.** The only difference was that it was covered in fallen leaves from a giant elm that was in the process of dropping its leaves for the winter - the car clearly hadn't been moved in over a week. I remember being oddly touched by that and thinking to myself, "man, the end of an era..."

You guys just don't get it[22]

This was in 2007 right when the first iPhone came out. Given that their store had opened directly across the street from the existing Palo Alto Apple Store on University Avenue, a lot of people were curious as to what Helio did and how their product compared to the iPhone. One day the manager noticed a guy wearing a black turtleneck, blue jeans, and glasses staring at the "Helio: don't call it a phone" window display outside the store for quite some time. When the manager came out to ask if he could help him or give him a demo of the product inside, the guy in the black turtleneck stuck his head in and peered into the store, but deliberately did not set his foot inside. It took some time, but finally he responded to the manager by shaking his head and saying the words **"You guys just don't get it, do you..."** and continued walking down the street. The manager had no idea who this guy was and thought nothing of it.

Two weeks later, the same manager was inside the store giving a demo of the amazing Helio smartphone to customers when he was interrupted by someone at the door. It was the same guy in the black turtleneck and blue jeans. "You guys STILL just don't get it, do you???" the guy said in an elevated voice from the entrance of the store. Before the manager could respond, the guy was gone again.

The manager was annoyed and said to customers "Who is this guy and who the hell does he think he is???"

"That's the founder of Apple," replied the customers.

Suffice to say, Helio moved out of the retail store only a year later, replaced by a much more popular Lululemon store.

Rare Breed[23]

I wasn't lucky enough to meet him, but when my IPOD stopped working, I went to the Apple shop in Amsterdam to complain. They regretted to inform me that the warranty was 1 week out of date, so they couldn't help me.

I wrote an email to customer service complaining about this, and CC'd Steve.jobs, jobs.steve@Apple.com and a couple of other variants.

About a week later I had a call from America from a customer service guy, who said 'Steve Jobs asked me to help you with your IPOD'. For the next month or so this guy called me every few of days to follow up until I got a replacement IPOD!

What a rare breed of man.

Mac-for-Shoes[24]

~10 years ago, my dad was in the united lounge working away on his Mac while he waited for a flight. A guy walks up to him and asks him what he uses his Mac for, and he replies that he uses it to design shoes for the company he's starting. The guy thinks that's neat, they chat about his start up, and gets around to mentioning that hey, his boss Steve Jobs is also in the lounge and would he like to meet him?

So yeah, **they did a Mac-for-shoes exchange or something and later someone sent my dad a photo with Jobs wearing Keens (The Mac Observer).** That was back in 2003 or so, around when Keen had just launched. Yup.

Apple Rule number One[25]

I worked at the Apple Store Pasadena for a while. We had just opened the store like a week or two prior. One day we were told that Steve Jobs was coming to visit.

Our store was the first in a complete redesign of the Apple Store. (Anyone remember the white kidney shaped tables at the original Stores?) There's a full scale replica Apple Store in Apple Retail's buildings in Cupertino, CA... But I guess he wanted to see it live.

Anyhow, it's ALL HANDS ON DECK... not a single thing was to be off from the planogram, etc. We were all assigned to keep our zones SPOTLESS. And most importantly, **we were told NOT TO APPROACH STEVE. (This is kind of Apple rule number 1, especially on campus in Cupertino**).

So Steve comes in... With full entourage. He's basically checking everything out... spends time talking with his people. I'm up front with iBook's and iMacs trying my absolute best to pretend not to watch his every move. He gets all the way around, and he's walking toward me. And I'm getting really nervous.

All of a sudden I catch glimpse of THE BIGGEST HOLE in a pair of jeans that I've ever seen. And there's a HUGE PATCH OF THIGH showing. And I'm trying my best to pretend to not notice...

He comes up to me, which I wasn't expecting, and extends his hand... having other things on my mind, like "don't act weird!", I stammer the words: "THANK YOU" just as he's saying, "Thank you." to me. He gave me a millisecond of look... the "that was weird" look... and went on his way. He was only in the store for about 10-15 minutes.

Asshole[26]

Prior to his return to Apple, it was obvious that the company was in trouble. Larry Ellison had floated the idea of a hostile takeover of the company, but it seemed to some of us Apple watchers that then-CEO Gil Amelio's turnaround plan might work.

I wrote an impassioned email to Steve at Pixar, pleading with him to find something else to do with his time. "Please," I implored him, "don't come back to Apple, you'll ruin it."

At the time, I really thought Steve and Larry were just twisting the knife into an already struggling company. As I made my living on Macs, I wanted the company to survive and not be distracted by Steve and Larry's games.

Shortly thereafter, Steve emailed me. He explained what he was trying to do, and that he was trying to save Apple.

And then he wrote the words I'll never forget:

"You may be right. But if I succeed, remember to look in the mirror and call yourself an asshole for me."

Consider it done, Steve. I could not have been more mistaken.

Printers Café Coffee[27]

I worked at Apple from 2005-2010. But the most memorable encounter I had with him was last summer in Palo Alto. A co-worker and I had just finished eating at Palo Alto Sol when my friend pointed out that Steve was just getting up from the table behind us and leaving. As we were also leaving we ended up following him at some distance -- as it was our habit to get coffee before going back to work, **we ducked into Printers Cafe and Steve was already in there**, peering at the pastry counter picking out a few pastries, taking his time. He seemed like he was just out enjoying the day -- he said "you wanna go ahead?" to which I replied, "No that's alright, you were here first -- we don't mind waiting." Or something like that. It was rather touching -- here's this guy, this icon we knew from over the years, his body clearly affected by his health issues, and he's happily picking out chocolate croissants and ordering a mocha. When he was done paying, he turned around and grinned, looking hard at both of us. That look -- so sharp and bright, curious and alive. He may have recognized us both from Apple - I thought he was going to say "hey I know you.." or something, but after a moment he just said "Thanks a lot, guys" or something to that effect, and wished us a good day. The words didn't really stick with me, but the smile and the direct look I'll remember. He was so close to the end at that point but yet still so present. I miss him, but I'm glad I have that memory to temper some of the ones from Apple.

Gas Cap Dangling[28]

It was hard not to run into Steve Jobs if you spent any time in downtown Palo Alto. While I never had a conversation with him, my chance encounters reminded me just how human this innovator was.

Once, I drove up behind his car on the way to Whole Foods. (Pretty easy to spot his car, especially with his "license plate." As I drove up behind him, I could see the gas cap dangling from the side of his car. I tried to grab my phone to snap a picture before deciding that stalking him as he went into Whole Foods would be bad. Chalked it up to a mad genius sometimes forgetting the small stuff.

A month later, driving by his house, glanced to see his car parked out front and the **GAS CAP DANGLING AGAIN.**

Loved it. Not because it had some profound effect on me, but just because it showed me we're all human. Even the brightest of us all.

Rollercoaster of Life[29]

In the early 1990s I was at a computer trade show and stopped at a corner booth near a rarely used entrance/exit door. The buzz was much further down the pavilion floor, and Steve Jobs was the only person in the NEXT booth.

For what felt like an eternity but must have been about 20 minutes, he demonstrated every feature and aspect of NEXT. He was incredibly passionate and persuasive, and I soon felt like I really wanted one, but at the same time I almost felt sorry for him. He must have run through this a thousand times. In this whole, huge show I was the only one listening.

Our conversation widened enough to discover people we knew in common from Campbell High School, but he was largely focussed on winning me over to his operating system. Eventually he reluctantly and graciously let me go.

I left with impression of someone whose circumstances were greatly diminished since his Apple days, yet who lived dynamically in the present and was focussed on creating a better future. In that moment I was his future, and the energy of his vision that he poured into me was memorable.

Having seen how determined he was when he was down, I was not surprised that he found a way back up again. **He was an example I've remembered each time the rollercoaster of life tosses me down and challenges me to get back up.**

Dined at Biological Father's Restaurant[30]

I can't imagine a better story than this one, and I think you'll agree:

Steve Jobs dined at his biological father's restaurant for years without either of them knowing who the other was.

They met, shook hands and spoke to one another on at least a couple of occasions. Steve's sister, who later figured out that the owner was their father, informed Steve, who made her promise not to tell the restaurant owner about him.

She rekindled her relationship with her estranged father, who liked to go on about how popular his old restaurant was, at one point saying, "Even Steve Jobs ate there! He was a great tipper!"

Quarter[31]

I bumped into Steve at the Palo Alto Whole Foods near both of our homes. He was in front of me in line paying for his groceries. It was the express checkout and he was wearing his traditional black turtle-neck. This was back in the early 2000s.

Here was a very wealthy, smart guy arguing with the cashier about what the correct change was for his purchase. He was demanding that he got another quarter ($0.25) for his change. This discussion went on for several minutes and held up the line so much that everyone behind him (including us) were getting annoyed.

I guess Steve had to be right. The cashier gave him a quarter and he walked away.

Excel[32]

In 1985, shortly after the original Mac was introduced, Steve Jobs gave a lunch time presentation at a local hotel to 1,000 folks attending a teacher's association conference in Edmonton, AB. The presentation was outstanding. He opened with an upbeat video of Apple's latest achievements. The soundtrack was the Pointer Sisters "I'm so excited". The room was pumped. He talked about imagination. He talked about what he saw as the future of computers and I remember distinctly his talking about how in the future there will be software that will allow us to explore molecules by zooming into them and rotating around their structures in a completely visual way. It was fantastic.

I had to get back to work so I headed out of the hotel into a nearby hotel where my car was parked. I pressed the button for the elevator, the doors opened and there was ... Steve Jobs!

I told him how much I enjoyed his presentation and shook his hand. He asked me what I did and I told him I was an IT Consultant. He told me about this amazing software that Microsoft was working on called "Excel". It is going to be phenomenal and that I should check it out. I told him I would.

The elevator doors opened. I exited the elevator and said goodbye.

Storyteller[33]

I worked at NeXT the summer of 94. I was in the break room with 2 colleagues when Jobs walked in and started making a bagel. We were sitting at a table eating ours when he out of the blue asked us "Who is the most powerful person in the world?" I said Mandela since I had just been there as an international observer for the elections. **In his confident fashion he stated "NO...you are all wrong...the most powerful person in the world is the story teller." At this point I was thinking to myself "Steve,** I love you but there is a fine line between genius and loco. And I think I am witnessing this right now". Steve continued, "The storyteller sets the vision, values and agenda of an entire generation that is to come and Disney has a monopoly on the storyteller business. You know what? I am tired of that bullshit, I am going to be the next storyteller" and he walked out with his bagel.

Photo by Steve Jobs[34]

After leaving my job at Apple, I dropped in for lunch one day. I was exiting the main building, Infinite Loop One, and just ahead of me was Steve Jobs, walking with the usual spring in his step that never seemed to go away even as he started looking more frail. Bumping into Steve was a surprisingly common occurrence for such a large company as Apple.

Steve was heading towards a car parked next to the curb with its door open, waiting for him. The car was idling. A family was standing near the Apple sign outside the building, a common site for people to take photos on their pilgrimages to Apple.

The father turned to Steve as he passed close by and asked, "Excuse me, sir, would you mind taking our photo?"

Steve paused for a moment as an iPhone was extended to him, realizing that they didn't seem to know who he was. With a hint of enthusiasm, he said "Sure!" as he took the iPhone into his hands.

Steve took a great deal of care composing the photo, backing up a few steps several times, tapping the iPhone screen to lock focus, then said "Smile!" as he snapped the photo, grinning a little bit himself to encourage the family to follow suit.

He handed back the iPhone and they said "Thank you, sir" as Steve stepped into his car, closed the door, and was driven away. The family looked at the photo that Steve had taken and all agreed that it looked great. Then the iPhone was pocketed and they were on their way.

And that was last time I saw Steve Jobs (2011).

I was amazed by the event, and i still wonder if that family got to know who they met?

Laptop issue[35]

When the first Intel MacBook Pro came out I had an issue where the top of the laptop wasn't aligned and didn't sit flush when closed. I went back and forth with support for a long time and the issue didn't get resolved. **Finally after a month of frustration I emailed Steve directly. The next day I received a call from his admin. She took care of the problem immediately.** The next day Apple had an all-hands where Steve referenced a customer's email where the top of the laptop didn't sit flush and how the customer had emailed support multiple times with no resolution and how it was unacceptable. A friend who worked at Apple texted me during the all-hands and said Steve was talking about my laptop issue.

Steve Jobs tried holding Door[36]

I got hired to work at the Apple store in San Jose in 2010 and had my first day of training at Apple Corporate. It was time for lunch at Cafe Mac's, where all the engineers at Apple have lunch every day. Our trainers gave us a full disclosure that sometimes Steve Jobs has lunch at Cafe Mac's but it's very rare. However, if it does happen, not to freak out and to just leave him alone.

Me and my new co-workers went off to Cafe Mac's, sticking together because we were a little intimidated by the environment, afraid we were going to accidently do something or say something to offend the engineers. Suddenly, I started hearing a lot of chatter amongst my co-workers. I asked what the fuss was about and they said "Steve Jobs is in here getting lunch". Gulp.

While I was getting lunch, I did everything I could to avoid him. I made sure to be on the opposite side of the room from him because a) I am awkward as hell and will say something weird b) I am a clutz and afraid I will trip and spill my food in front of him.

I got my food and headed towards the door. **There were a couple of people walking in front of me. Someone was holding the door open for all of us, and it was Steve Jobs. I tried holding on to the door to let him and the people behind me pass. But he continued to hold on to the door, and like a kind gentlemen said, "No, after you" and then smiled at me.**

Best first day of work ever.

Steve Jobs Founded HP[37]

I met Steve Jobs once, it was not a setting involving business but a social setting.

We were at an ice skating rink in Palo Alto off of Middlefield Road.

I see a man casually watching his kids and talking to his wife, I lean over to my niece and say "...that is Steve Jobs, the man who founded Apple Computers."

Her step father overhears us, asks me why Steve Jobs was so important. I tell him the iconic facts about Apple and Pixar.

The Stepfather walks over to Steve and calmly says, "...I hear you are the guy who founded HP..."

Steve looks at him and said, "...nope..." and walks away.

Funniest and saddest thing to watch....

Fruit Juice[38]

The time was the 1970s; the place was Bombay, India. There was a little joint down the road from where I lived called Dipti's Fruit Juice, which served the best fresh fruit juice in town. It was also a very popular hippie hangout with, among other things, a notice board on which they could write personal messages (like "Guitar for sale" or "Chick wants lift to Kathmandu").

My friends and I used to go there regularly for the fruit juice, and also for the conversations we'd strike up with some of the hippies. One of them, I remember, was young guy with long dark hair and a scraggly beard we met a couple of times, who talked enthusiastically (and rather naively) about finding enlightenment in India. **One of my friends, who was an IIT engineer got into a conversation with him one day and told me that he was, surprisingly, an electronics genius (which belied his very hippie exterior). He told us he was from California, I remember, and that his name was Steve.**

Looking back, I sometimes wonder, was that guy - could he have been -Steve Jobs? I guess I will never know....

Dinner with Kids[39]

I saw Steve Jobs having dinner with his kids in early 2011 at Tomasso's Pizza in North Beach in San Francisco. My Dad and I were waiting for a table and I made eye contact with him several times as we waited for our table. **He seemed to be enjoying his meal with his family.** He was slouched in his chair while his kids were eating. He was rather thin.

He was wearing a hoodie and most people in the restaurant were eating as normal and nobody made a scene.

Those few moments I shared just in the same space as Steve Jobs came back to me at the time of his death and constantly as I read Walter Issacson's biography.

Free MacBook[40]

I asked him for a free MacBook Air back in May 2008. **He replied: Sorry, but no. - Steve**, sent from my iPhone.

Believing in yourself[41]

My friend once told me (I really don't know if it's true!) that, once he e-mailed Mr Jobs, asking a question- "What is more important than Apple Inc.?"
Then Mr Jobs answered- **"Believing in yourself!"**

At least it's Inspirational!

First Hour[42]

I met Steve Job in 2010 while being a summer intern. **It was my first hour in Apple** and I was looking for my manager. That was shock for me.

He asked me:

- what are you doing here?

Dinner at Sunnyvale[43]

About five years ago, one evening, just as I had sat down with my wife and daughter at Saravana Bhavan, a South Indian vegetarian restaurant in Sunnyvale, in walked Steve Jobs with his wife and son. They sat down on the table behind us.

So, it was with great amusement, we watched Steve raise his hand several times to attract the attention of the waiter, who summarily ignored him. As the only white guy in the restaurant, we thought he would be instantly recognized and served with special attention. Instead, he had the worst table in the house. A bored waiter passed plastic menu cards at his family without giving a second glance. Eventually, he did get served with the mass efficiency of an overworked staff. And, no one bothered him during his dinner either.

My wife and I observed in awe as Steve and his family enjoyed a quiet meal in the riotous, inexpensive place in the heart of Silicon Valley. It dawned on us that no one in the restaurant had recognized Steve in his low key attire and a stubble. At the end, when no one came to his table to present the check, Steve rose up, dropped a few cash notes on the table and walked out, as the server wiped his table.

Just then, the manager walked by, and I asked him, "Did you know that was Steve Jobs?" He smiled and gave me the Indian head shake - a cross between yes and no. To this day, I don't know what he meant.

DVD-Burning Program[44]

Mike Evangelist (yep, that's his name) still remembers one of his first meetings with Jobs. It took place in the Apple boardroom in early 2000, just a few months after Apple purchased the American division of Astarte, a German software company where Evangelist was an operations manager.

Phil Schiller, Apple's long-time head of marketing, put Evangelist on a team charged with coming up with ideas for a DVD-burning program that Apple planned to release on high-end Macs -- an app that would later become iDVD.

"We had about three weeks to prepare," Evangelist says. He and another employee went to work creating beautiful mock-ups depicting the perfect interface for the new program. On the appointed day, Evangelist and the rest of the team gathered in the boardroom. They'd brought page after page of prototype screenshots showing the new program's various windows and menu options, along with paragraphs of documentation describing how the app would work.

"Then Steve comes in," Evangelist recalls. "He doesn't look at any of our work. He picks up a marker and goes over to the whiteboard. He draws a rectangle. **'Here's the new application**,' he says. **'It's got one window. You drag your video into the window. Then you click the button that says BURN. That's it. That's what we're going to make**.' "

"We were dumbfounded," Evangelist says. This wasn't how product decisions were made at his old company. Indeed, this isn't how products are planned anywhere else in the industry.

I love this story because it shows that he really lived by his mantra: focus and simplicity (which can be seen in all Apple's products).

IPod Launch[45]

I read somewhere that the night before the iPod launch Steve Jobs was playing with one of the demo units and felt the headphone jack didn't feel solid enough when he plugged in the headphones. So he made the engineers stay up all night replacing the jacks on 100 demo units until they clicked right. I think about that every time I plug my headphones into my iPhone.

Correction: As Anand Rajaram pointed out in the comments, it was the original iPod launch.

Firing People[46]

"What have you done for Apple, lately?"

Everyone who has worked in the valley has heard this bit of folklore, over and over, again -- Jobs firing employee/s in the elevator. The closest description can found in Jobs' unofficial biography -- "The Second Coming of Steve Jobs".

Still, the Apple rank-and-file remained fearful of the Bad Steve persona. Word got around about Steve going into meetings, saying, **"This is shit," and firing people on the spot. People worried about getting trapped with him in an elevator for a few seconds, afraid that they might not have a job when the doors opened.** The reality was that Steve's summary executions were rare, but a handful of victims is enough to terrorize a whole company.

For a while there was an elevator in Steve's building that had protective coverings on its walls because construction was going on, and someone said: "This must be Steve's elevator since it's padded." Another employee responded: "Is it for him or for us?"

Intern Dancer[47]

I interned at Apple during the summer of 2006. Steve gave a talk and had a Q&A with our group. Here are some highlights:

- When asked whether Apple would ever make a car, Steve said that there were already some very good manufacturers out there (I'm pretty sure he mentioned BMW specifically), and also that it wouldn't make sense for Apple to get into the car business. He said that Apple was, however, working on making great new products, ending with the rhetorical question: **"How many of you love using your cell phone right now?"**

- An intern asked **"Can I be a dancer in the next iPod commercial?"** **Steve's response? "Show me what you got!"** The guy was called down onstage to bust some moves. Steve must have been impressed - he instructed an assistant to put the intern in touch with the right people to make it happen.

Steve Jobs Wish[48]

After my junior year of college I was able to finagle my way into an internship at Apple. I moved out to Sunnyvale, worked in Cupertino coding for an internal team and only passed by Steve Jobs a few times. He was always walking quickly, but would give eye contact and that brief half smile and head nod that strangers give each other.

I heard him speak in the executive lecture series, where all the Apple execs came in to talk to the interns. Steve took questions, and one was related to where he gets his inspiration from and he said half-jokingly "from the scorn of women" before giving a more complete answer. +1.

My one moment with Steve was in the cafeteria. I sat down for lunch and Steve was sitting behind me speaking to someone. It was hard to concentrate on whatever mundane conversation I having when there was sat a man with so much vision and wisdom that I wanted to learn from, just one table away. So I listened, and remember hearing him say:

I wish I could be a fly on the wall in 100 years to see what technology is like.

That sentence stuck with me for a long time. To me it symbolizes the type of long term thinking and resolve necessary to build an entity (company, organization, ideals, etc.) that is decades old. To create something that lives on for centuries and finds ways to impact our world in profound ways. Our incremental thinking in entrepreneurship must be balanced with a long term world view of what society should be like.

Bills[49]

This is a hard question to answer, because there are so many great stories.

One of my favourite ones, though, came when Jamis McNiven, founder of Bucks, told me about when he was a contractor working on Steve Jobs' house.

Jamis says he actually tackled Steve one day to get him to pay his bills. He told me that story early in this video:

Also, Jamis told me lots of stories about what a perfectionist Jobs is (they argued about how wires would be stapled in Jobs' garage, for instance, and in the video I shot he talked about a rattling door knob that drove Jobs' nuts). You can also hear Jamis tell me a bunch of Silicon Valley stories in that video.

Bucks, by the way, is where tons of VCs hang out and where Hotmail was incorporated.

Woz (aka Steve Wozniak, Apple co-founder), pictured above next to an Apple II at the Computer History Museum, told me lots of stories about Jobs. I remember the first time I interviewed Woz. It was the day after Jobs released the first NeXT computer. I asked Woz what he thought about it. He told me "I've learned not to say anything if I can't say something nice."

He told me stories of how Atari paid Steve Jobs $5,000 to develop the game "Breakout" and Jobs told Woz that he only got paid $500. Woz forgave him, though, and said he would have designed the game for free.

Machines[50]

I left Macromedia in the winter of 1991. About a month later I get a call from Jobs - **asking me to develop for the NeXT machine.**

I tell him: "Steve - we developed for a B&W Steve Jobs machine once before. When the NeXT is in colour - give me a call."

Jobs then asks me "what are you going to do?" And I tell him that I'm consulting with Intel, Sony, JVC and Fujitsu" and he tells me "be careful you might turn into a dickhead".

:-)

Tough Time at Apple[51]

From John Lilly's blog:

It turns out that I worked at Apple ATG (Advanced Technology Group) in 1994/5 when I was a grad student at Stanford, and then again for all of 1997, when I moved back here from Trilogy.

I remember being at a talk he gave shortly after returning in 1997 as Interim CEO. A bunch of us employees (I was at ATG at the time) were in Town Hall in Building 4 at Infinite Loop to hear him, and he was fired up. Talked a lot about how Apple was going to completely turn things around and become great.

It was a tough time at Apple — we were trading below book value on the market — our enterprise value was actually less than our cash on hand. And the rumours were everywhere that we were going to be acquired by Sun. Someone in the audience asked him about Michael Dell's suggestion in the press a few days previous that Apple should just shut down and return the cash to shareholders,n**and as I recall, Steve's response was: "Fuck Michael Dell."** Good god, what a message from a CEO! He followed it up by admitting that the stock price was terrible (it was under $10, I think — pretty sure it was under $2 split-adjusted), and that what they were going to do was reissue everyone's options on the low price, but with a new 3 year vest. He said, explicitly: **"If you want to make Apple great again, let's get going. If not, get the hell out."** I think it's not an overstatement to say that just about everyone in the room loved him at that point.

Google Glasses[52]

I was a graduate intern at Apple during the summer of 2007. That's right, the same summer the iPhone launched. What a time to be there.

As part of the internship program (which, by the way, is an incredible operation) every couple weeks we were given access to a VP from a different department. When I say "given access," I mean that a different VP gave a talk about their field of expertise to an audience of about 250 interns. This was followed by a Q&A.

Even though he wasn't a VP, Steve Jobs always did one of these talks.

I honestly don't remember what he talked about. Chalk it up to the reality distortion field. But I do remember one moment during the Q&A session. A young guy in the front row raised his hand, and Steve called on him.

"Yeah, I have an idea for a product, but I don't think anyone will listen to it," the kid said.

Brief pause. "Go ahead," said Steve. "I'm listening."

An awkward laugh rippled across the auditorium. Then we all realized he was serious.

The kid stumbled and stuttered and finally described an idea that I vaguely recall as resembling what has since been embodied as Google Glasses.

Steve very politely shot it down.

That was the thing about him. I saw this more than once: He could rip someone a new ***hole, and at the end of it, they would feel better for it. They would simply say, "thank you."

Willing to start again[53]

Ron Johnson (Apple Retail Store VP) recently said on a talk at Stanford 'The biggest lesson I can recall from Steve is that **you have to be willing to start all over again.**"

He remembers one of the final days while designing the Apple Retail Stores.

'Steve I have been thinking and I think our stores are designed all wrong. We organized the store products. But if Apple's is going to organize around activities like music and movies, well, the store should be organized around music and movies and things you do"

Which Steve answered "Do you know how big a change this is?! I don't have time to redesign the store. You might be right... but I don't want you to say word about it to anybody because I don't know if I want to do that."

They both drove 2 miles to a meeting with the Apple Store design and architects team, about 20 people. Steve didn't say a word to Ron after saying that.

When they arrive Steve immediately says "Well, Ron thinks our store is all wrong. And he's right, so I'm going to leave now. And Ron, you work with the team and design the store."

He later called back Ron "This reminded me something I've learn from every move at Pixar. It's not about speed to market. It's really about doing your level best."

Biology and Technology[54]

Steve Jobs was discussing with his biographer Walter Isaacson his life: "after Jobs was diagnosed with cancer, Reed (his son) began spending his summer working in a Stanford oncology lab.... One very few silver linings about me getting sick is that Reed`s gotten to spend a lot of time studying with some very good doctors, Jobs said. His enthusiasms for it is exactly how I felt about computers when I was his age. **I think the biggest innovations of the twenty-first century will be the intersection of biology and technology.** A new era is beginning, just like the digital one when I was his age."

No bullshit[55]

My favourite is after the iPhone team worked for months on what the product would be, had a lengthy presentation ready for Jobs, with all the details and tech, and he just walked in the room, drew a simple image on the board, showed the screen and interface and said that's what it should be. Done. **No bullshit.**

Plane Ticket[56]

I found this one from Steve Wozniak's website (woz.org). Not many people know this. It happened while Steve Jobs was in India, and Woz mentioned it in one of the letters on his site:

Around that time Steve went to India and ran into someone who had lost their plane ticket home. **Steve actually gave that person his own ticket**. Steve had no money but trusted the person to replace it, and sure enough the replacement was mailed to him and he got home.

Shave my Head[57]

Playboy: Where you shaved your head.

Jobs: That's not quite the way it happened. I was walking around in the Himalayas and I stumbled onto this thing that turned out to be a religious festival. There was a baba, a holy man, who was the holy man of this particular festival, with his large group of followers. I could smell good food. I hadn't been fortunate enough to smell good food for a long time, so I wandered up to pay my respects and eat some lunch. For some reason, this baba, upon seeing me sitting there eating, immediately walked over to me and sat down and burst out laughing. He didn't speak much English and I spoke a little Hindi, but he tried to carry on a conversation and he was just rolling on the ground with laughter. Then he grabbed my arm and took me up this mountain trail. It was a little funny, because here were hundreds of Indians who had travelled for thousands of miles to hang out with this guy for ten seconds and I stumble in for something to eat and he's dragging me up this mountain path. We get to the top of this mountain half an hour later and there's this little well and pond at the top of this mountain, and he dunks my head in the water and pulls out a razor from his pocket and starts to shave my head. I'm completely stunned. I'm 19 years old, in a foreign country, up in the Himalayas, and here is this bizarre Indian baba who has just dragged me away from the rest of the crowd, **shaving my head atop this mountain peak**. I'm still not sure why he did it.

Surprising People[58]

Givens recalled one day when a secretary was late, and Jobs demanded to know why.

"(She was a) single mom, good secretary," Givens said. "She said, 'My car wouldn't start.' So, that afternoon, (Jobs) walks into her office, throws a set of keys to a brand new Jaguar and says, 'Here, don't be late anymore.' **He was always doing things like that, surprising people**."

Near to Death[59]

He almost died in a plane crash.

(Summarized from Jobs and Intel's Noyce Forged Early Bond)
It was 1980, when Bob Noyce was the chairman of Intel and Steve was a young 20s. Steve often showed up in Bob's house, asking for advice in life and his young company Apple. Despite being sceptical with his vision, Bob enjoyed hanging around with Steve, often taking him on his personal airplane (Bob could fly on his own until near his death).

Jobs became animated describing the flight on Noyce's new plane. After landing on Lake Tahoe, Noyce flew back to the San Jose airport but forgot to lock in the wheels and the plane landed nose-down with sparks flying. **"I was picturing the headline: 'Bob Noyce and Steve Jobs Killed in Fiery Plane Crash,'"** Jobs told her. "It was only due to his excellent piloting that we survived."

Bluetooth[60]

My youngest brother has muscular dystrophy and is now quadriplegic, with just about enough movement to steer his electric wheelchair. A few years ago my mom found that someone had put together a Bluetooth computer controller allowing the user to control the computer using the wheelchair joystick.

The only problem was that the mouse move juddered, pausing then racing across the screen to catch up with the movement, rendering the whole set up useless. A lot of testing later, showed that it worked perfectly on a Windows PC, just failed on the iMac. **My mom spent a lot of very frustrating time talking to Apple support here in the UK, who essentially said that it was an unapproved Bluetooth device and tough luck we were on our own.**

Out of sheer frustration my mom wrote an email to Steve Jobs venting her frustration at what was happening, never expecting a reply. The surprise was a remarkably prompt, somewhat curt reply from him. He had assigned a group of technicians and programmers to resolve the problem.

This brief interaction with Steve Jobs resulted in an effect that changed my brother's life and had a huge, wonderful effect on my family. We never thought a CEO of a corporate would care. He did, he didn't have to, but he diverted resources to make a difference to just one person, the difference between dependence and independence in a number of important ways. Thank you never seemed enough for what was done and for all he did in the corporate world and all of the incredible things he introduced to the world it is for this one act of human kindness he will forever be in the heart of me and my family.

iTunes[61]

The story of the time we met Steve Jobs (and a boardroom full of Apple VPs):

Before iTunes, we wrote one of the Mac's first MP3 jukebox apps; Audion. We were personally asked by Steve if we wanted to "throw in" with Apple on what we now know to be iTunes. We declined and somehow don't have any major regrets, but we can only wonder how different our lives might have been.

Emeryville[62]

This is hearsay, but I've heard it a few times the same way. When Pixar was first building in Emeryville, Steve and co had to present the plans to city council for approval. Emeryville, especially at the time, was not the nicest place in the world and sits near a rough section of Oakland. Even earlier this year, the Oaks Card Club down the street from Pixar's main gate was raided by the FBI.

After Pixar presented its plans, a council member said something like, "Mr Jobs, you're building this beautiful campus with these amazing trees but then putting a big, ugly fence around it. **Why not open it and share it with the citizens of Emeryville?**"

Steve replied with, "Apparently you're unfamiliar with the notion of private property."

Graphical UI[63]

In the early 80's Steve visited Carnegie Mellon a lot, getting us to buy Macs. One day we gave him a demo of **a graphical UI we were creating for the Andrew system**. He said, "I get it. This is kind of funky," and he didn't mean that in a good way. I guess he would have made us do it over or worse, if we'd been working for him. At the time, I made the usual engineer's rationalizations--it was still under development, we'd fix it later, etc. Now I know better.

Protocol[64]

As a new Apple employee, after orientation, you get your first and only free lunch with your new manager. So there I am, with my shiny new employee badge, standing in line to pay, having decided upon pizza vs sushi or one of the other delicious options.

So I'm just looking around all nonchalantly, when BOOM who strolls into my field of view had an odd gait, kind of springy, even when he was at the peak of health **but STEVE JOBS. OMG. STAY COOL.** He's right there, not 20 feet away!

Wait a second. He's headed my way. I look back at the cashier to assess the sitch. Couple people in front of me ; no way I pay and skidaddle before he closes that distance.

So now it's decision time. What's the protocol here? Is he going to want cuts? There are like 6 people behind me. Is that the deal? Does SJ get automatic cuts? If so is it frontiers or back cuts? What if he asks what I do? I heard he fired a guy for answering that wrong. I don't want to be fired on my first day!**GEEZ HE IS Like THREE FEET AWAY NOW**

So naturally, I peel out of line and head over to the frozen treat freezer as if I forgot to grab an It's It. Which in this case I had forgotten. Anyway. While I'm over there laying low, I look back; Steve is now selecting an Odwalla bar or something from the case next to the cash register. Which was where he'd been heading, and what he'd been looking at, all along.

And that was the first time I encountered Steve at Apple, on my first day. I never did find out what the cuts protocol was.

Autobiography of a Yogi[65]

At a recent Self-Realization Fellowship Sunday morning service, Brother Bhumananda, a Self-Realization Fellowship minister, said that a few years back the phone rang up at Self Realization headquarters (in Los Angeles).

The caller said, "This is Steve Jobs." The person answering initially thought it was a prank call, but it really was Steve Jobs calling personally to say, **"I want to get permission to put 'Autobiography of a Yogi' on iTunes. It's my favourite book!"**

Steve Jobs said that he had read 'Autobiography of a Yogi' over 30 times. It was the first audio-book to become available on ITunes.

Steve Jobs Prediction[66]

In the very early '80s, Bob Noyce convinced Steve Jobs to join him on the board of trustees for Grinnell College, where I attended college and worked on the school paper. I heard that Steve was coming to town for a meeting and managed to schedule an interview for the Scarlet & Black. Steve was enthusiastic and engaging and we ended up conducting the interview while wandering the residential neighbourhoods of Grinnell -- tree lined streets, big porches, lilacs blooming all around. It turned out that we grew up in the same hometown and, even though he was 6 years older than I was, we swam on the same city swim team.

After the 90 minute interview, **I wrote up a long and exuberant article about how Steve and his personal computers were going to change the world.** Then I burst in on my favorite Economics professor to tell him all about it. My professor summed up his scepticism with one pithy phrase: "It'll never happen." Oh but it did Professor Bloch -- and even faster with more impact than Steve predicted at the time.

That night happened to be the night of our school waltz, and Steve showed up. He was wearing cowboy boots and I tried to teach him how to waltz, to no avail. He drifted away that night and I saw him about a year later for another interview, at which point he wasn't nearly as accessible.

He had such confidence that he was right, that he was onto something big; his confidence in his vision was as important as the vision itself.

No Skills[67]

Gamasutra has some great stories about Steve here in "Steve Jobs, Atari Employee Number 40" by Frank Cifaldi.

An excerpt:

"He was this real scuzzy kid," Alcorn once told video game historian Steven Kent. "I think I said, 'We should either call the cops or we should talk to him.' So I talked to him."

Jobs had no real engineering experience to bring to the table. He had a small amount of education from Reed College, but it was in a completely unrelated major, and he had dropped out early. But he had a way with words, seemed to have a passion for technology, and probably lied about having worked at Hewlett-Packard.

**"I figured, this guy's gotta be cheap, man. He really doesn't have much
skills at all," Alcorn remembers. "So I figured I'd hire him."**

Come back[68]

I cried when Jobs came back, and I don't cry.

For me the biggest moment was when Jobs came back to Apple. I had been an Apple fan since the first Mac in 1984. I loved the linear address space of the Motorola processor as much as the mature GUI. Unfortunately Microsoft closed the gap over the years, and by the mid-90s I had stopped recommending Macs to friends even though I still used them. Remember Dell's suggestion to liquidate Apple?

During the 1990s I spent a LOT of time on the CompuServe Mac forums discussing how the Mac could stay relevant. These forums discussed Apple's HW & SW future, and Apple's OS strategy had been a mess for years: check out Taligent's history. **My Apple moment happened while reading the Mac forum one night in 1996 a few hours after the announcement that Apple was buying Next and Jobs was coming back. Using Next to solve the OS problems was completely unexpected and not even rumoured at the time. I clearly remember staring at the post (just text in those days) as a single tear of joy rolled down my left cheek.**

My only hope at the time was that Apple's market share might be able to get up to 5%. Even Apple's greatest fans couldn't imagine that Apple under Jobs would dominate like they have.

Job Offer[69]

In 1985, on the day after he was fired by the board, he came into the Softwaire Centre, then at 477 University Ave. in Palo Alto. He walked around to check out new software and how it was displayed as he and folks from the early Mac team, and local Mac hw and sw folks often did, and purchased a square black packaged game or simulator called "Millionaire" with his credit card, for $49.95.

The next day, the owner of the store was reconciling the cc receipts before going to the bank and **asked if Steve had come in to apply for the p/t sales position or the p/t stock position.** I said "huh" and he wryly pointed to the front door where we had a piece of paper for job openings taped.

16 years later, the first PA Apple store would occupy that space (including where the old Swains House of Music, and a deli, used to stand).

Torvalds to Apple[70]

I read a lot about Steve Jobs.

Around 2000, Apple founder Steve Jobs invited Linus Torvalds to Apple's Cupertino campus and offered him a job at Apple. Torvalds rejected the job, of course, and refused to work on 'non-Linux' things. Read more and know how it happened.

In an old interview with Wired, Linus Torvalds said that around 2000 Steve Jobs invited him to Apple's Cupertino campus and tried to recruit him on his Unix-based kernel.

"UNIX for the biggest user base: that was the pitch," Torvalds says.

So, what was Torvalds' reply? He said no, obviously.

Linus already hated Mac OS's Mach kernel. Besides, Steve wanted Linus to drop Linux development and start doing non-Linux stuff — a big NO for Linus.

In 2000, Apple was yet to ship the first version of OS X 10.0. At that time, Apple had heavily invested in Mac OS X that later became a building block of the long list of iDevices.

Well, what if Torvalds would have accepted Steve Jobs' proposal?

Google Second O[71]

In 2008, Steve Jobs called Vic Gundotra, a Google Engineer back then, who handled all Mobile Applications, on a Sunday, to tell him that the **second O in the Google logo didn't have the right shade of yellow.**

"So Vic," he said, "We have an urgent issue, one that I need addressed right away. I've already assigned someone from my team to help you, and I hope you can fix this tomorrow."

"I've been looking at the Google logo on the iPhone and I'm not happy with the icon. **The second O in Google doesn't have the right yellow gradient.** It's just wrong and I'm going to have Greg fix it tomorrow. Is that okay with you?"

Remembering the incident Gundotra once said, "When I think about leadership, passion and attention to detail, I think back to the call I received from Steve Jobs on a Sunday morning in January. It was a lesson I'll never forget. CEOs should care about details. Even shades of yellow. On a Sunday."

Tagline[72]

I LOVE APPLE

Remember the **Original iPod** that was released in 2001? The one with the iconic mechanical scroll wheel?

It was Apple's one of the most influential, profitable and innovative invention which soon became a flagship product.

SO HOW THIS IS A GREAT STORY OF STEVE JOBS RIGHT?

Steve Jobs famously created a tagline for the iPod it goes like,

It carries a thousand songs and goes right in my pocket.(In those days it was a big thing)

SO WHAT'S SO GREAT ABOUT THIS?

about 3 months before the iPod launched and made its mark, an employee came to Steve Jobs to show him the final prototype, Steve found it 'too fat' and told the employee to make it slimmer/thinner. The employee told that he couldn't make it any thinner than it already was. Steve then took the iPod's ONLY prototype and dropped it into an aquarium, on doing so a large bubble came out, Steve then told

"Look, there's this bubble coming out, it means there's air in that thing. NOW GO REDUCE IT! "

If Steve hadn't reduced the thickness of the iPod, I don't think he would ever have such a grin on his face when saying "a thousand songs and goes right into your pocket"

When I actually think about it, I can't help but admire his awesome presence of mind. I mean who drops the only prototype in a bloody water tank! Just to make it a little thinner?

ONLY CRAZY PEOPLE!**And those who are crazy enough to think they can change the world are the ones who do!**

Two questions[73]

One of my friends did an internship at Apple. Apparently Apple has a day where the interns get to meet Steve Jobs (this was obviously a few years back) and ask him questions. Two questions that were asked stuck in her mind.

1. "What do you wish for the most?"

Steve Jobs: "I wish people would stop asking me stupid questions."

2. "What do you do in your free time?"

Steve Jobs: **"I fuck my wife."**

Recently, I interviewed with a mid/upper-level manager at Apple for a hardware position. I asked him what he thought about Steve Jobs. He thought for a while, looked at me seriously, and said very carefully, "I respect Steve. He's a great man and absolutely brilliant, but I would not want to be his friend."

Sculley's words[74]

There's his classic pitch to John Sculley when recruiting him to run Apple. **In Sculley's words:** "And then he looked up at me and just stared at me with the stare that only Steve Jobs has and he said do you want to sell sugar water for the rest of your life or do you want to come with me and change the world and I just gulped because I knew I would wonder for the rest of my life what I would have missed."

Steve Job's Last words[75]

An eye for an eye only ends up making whole world blind!

Steve Job's Last words:

"I reached pinnacle of success in the business world. In other's eyes my life is an epitome of success.
However, aside from work, I have little joy. In the end wealth is only a fact of life I am accustomed to.
At this moment I am lying on death bed recalling my whole life, I realise that all the recognition and wealth I took so much pride in, have paled and become meaningless in the face of impending death.

In the darkness, I look at the green lights from the life supporting machines and hear the humming mechanical sounds, I can feel the breath of God and of death drawing closer, Now I know, when we have accumulated sufficient wealth to last our lifetime, we should pursue other matters that are unrelated to wealth...Should be something that is more important: Perhaps relationships, perhaps art, perhaps a dream from younger days ...Non-stop pursuing of wealth will only turn a person into a twisted being, just like me.

God gave us the senses to let us feel the love in everyone's heart, not the illusions brought about by wealth. The wealth I have won in my life I cannot bring with me.
What I can bring is only the memories precipitated by love.

That's the true riches which will follow you, accompany you, giving you strength and light to go on.
Love can travel a thousand miles. Life has no limit. Go where you want to go. Reach the height you want to reach. It is all in your heart and in your hands.
What is the most expensive bed in the world? – "Sick bed" ...

Real Facts[76]

1. **Once, Steve Jobs started believing that if he ate too many apples, he wouldn't need to take a bath.** After a few days, people started complaining about the bad smell coming from him. At first, he wouldn't agree and would argue but later, he got the point.

2. **Steve Jobs used to wear a 1000 USD Porsche Watch which he would give to anyone who appreciated its design.** After a few minutes, he would have a new piece of the same watch on his hand.

3. **Steve Jobs used to ride a BMW bike** and he liked its design so much that he put it in a showcase at.

4. **Once Steve Jobs went to his real biological father's restaurant without both of them knowing the true relation between them.** When Steve talked with Mona Simpson, his real biological sister, he mentioned that the place had great food. When Mona Simpson met their real biological father Abdulfattah Jandali, he told her that Steve Jobs had been at his restaurant once. In this way, Mona figured out that the duo have already met.

Out of Respect[77]

Here are a few that I feel worth sharing.

- A lawyer gave her biological sister "Mona Simpson" call to inform that her **"long-lost brother"** was rich and famous and wanted to contact her. The lawyer refused to tell her his Name, and her friends started **betting-pool** on who he may be.
  And the man who came to meet her was - Steve Jobs

- When he got kicked out of Apple, he told his sister about a dinner at which 500 Silicon Valley leaders met with the **then-sitting president** and Steve wasn't invited.
- Tim Cook and he had a great friendship and Cook even offered him part of his own liver to try and Save Job's life.
- His office remains almost completely **untouched** since his death. **Tim Cook** and his team decided to **keep his office as a form of memorial** with his **nameplate still hung outside door.**
  And nothing beats this:

  When he died Google, Samsung and many other companies postponed their big announcements out of Respect.

We knew each other by sight[78]

A bunch of us were in the old screening room in Point Richmond with Steve early the morning of the Pixar IPO. **We were watching the financial news for that PIXR ticker to go by.** So we witnessed the moment that Steve became a billionaire. Quite the payoff for $50 million and almost a decade of hanging in there.

He didn't say anything. No fist pumps or whoops. But I've never seen him happier. That was one beaming smile.

The Impossible, make it Smaller[79]

When engineers working on the very first iPod completed the prototype, they presented their work to Steve Jobs for his approval. Jobs played with the device, scrutinized it, weighed it in his hands, and promptly rejected it. It was too big.

The engineers explained that they had to **reinvent inventing to create the iPod, and that it was simply impossible to make it any smaller**. Jobs was quiet for a moment. Finally he stood, walked over to an aquarium, and dropped the iPod in the tank. After it touched bottom, bubbles floated to the top.

"Those are air bubbles," he snapped. "That means there's space in there. Make it smaller."

Comeback[80]

Steve Jobs and Steve Wozniak were friends who together started **Apple** back in 70's. Wozniak was the inventor and he invented the Apple computer and Jobs went out to sell it and got the company going. Apple, even in those times, was a pioneer of design and technology. The company did wonderfully well in the initial years and its IPO (Initial Public Offering) was the bigger ever in American history after Ford Motor Company. Steve Jobs was a millionaire many times over even in his twenties and the head of one of the coolest computer companies in the World.

But then, things began to go wrong. Steve Jobs apparently started creating an internal conflict among the employees of Apple. **The board was not too happy with him and they decided to remove him from the company. Imagine, the guy started Apple, sustained it through all those initial hard years , put his life into the company and six years later, just like that , they threw him out!**

Not one to give up, he went on to start another company called **NeXT,** paving way for some of the most cutting edge technology of its time. He also launched a computer animation company along with NeXT.

So, here's the deal, this guy gets chucked out of his first company, starts a new one and few years later sells this company to the first company he originally founded. And you know how much he sold NeXT to Apple for? Five **hundred million dollars!** That automatically brought Steve Jobs back into the board of Apple and few years later he became the CEO and the rest, as you all know, is HISTORY.

Steve Jobs life is an inspiration to every person, who aspire for greatness.

Gorilla Glass[81]

I like the story where Wozniak + Jobs re-designed some Atari ICs and they wanted to split the earning. Jobs got $5000 from Atari but told Woz, he only got $700 and thus earned $4650 for swinging the whip behind Woz who did most of the work.

Steve Jobs himself made the decision to switch the original iPhone's screen from plastic to glass at the last minute due to a scratching issue. In his biography by Walter Isaacson(on iBook's here), Jobs is said to have called Corning Glass CEO Wendell Weeks directly to request that the company begin making its **Gorilla Glass** product again.

"We don't have the capacity," Weeks replied. "None of our plants make the glass now." "Don't be afraid," Jobs replied. This stunned Weeks, who was good-humoured and confident but not used to Jobs reality distortion field. He tried to explain that a false sense of confidence would not overcome engineering challenges, but that was a premise that Jobs had repeatedly shown he didn't accept. He stared at Weeks unblinking. "Yes, you can do it," he said. "Get your mind around it. You can do it."

Weeks retold this story, he shook his head in astonishment. "We did it in under six months," he said. "We produced a glass that had never been made." Corning's facility in Harrisburg, Kentucky, which had been making **LCD displays, was converted almost overnight to make gorilla glass full-time. "We put our best scientists and engineers on it, and we just made it work."** In his airy office, Weeks has just one framed memento on display. It's a message Jobs sent the day the iPhone came out: "We couldn't have done it without you."

Apology[82]

Back in 1993 I was the NeXT distributor in Mexico. After many struggles I managed to sell a 1 million dollar deal to a bank in Mexico.

The owner of the bank demanded that Steve came to Mexico in order to sign the contract, which seemed like a deal breaker.

Strangely enough, Steve accepted.

HP was the hardware provider to the bank and has just signed an alliance with NeXT to have NeXT Step running on their wonderful PA Risc workstations.

Having heard of Steve coming to Mexico to sign the contract, HP organized an event catering to the financial services and got Steve to deliver a Keynote on the event.

I did try to contact the VP and he wouldn't return my calls, but ended up working with his team the details for the presentation and organizing the million details that Steve demanded in a hotel and specially his meals.

I had been in a couple of meetings with Steve and had no hope he would recognize me in a meeting, neither the NeXT people thought so.

What we never expected was that Steve came to the Lobby and without hesitation (and being followed closely by HP´s VP) walk directly to me and deliver a life changing sentence:

"I know you have helped us here to get this contract and we are here to deliver, thank you so much for your help, we will never forget"

I was 25 at the time and was speechless.

Steve already was my heroes, but what really overwhelmed me is that he could recognize me and could thank me.

It was so clear to me the difference between the two guys, and I had not forgotten ever since.

It was a very clear lesson and had nothing to do with technology.

Apple fest[83]

I am writing a book about my 30-year friendship with Steve Jobs and his spirit...

Okay...I have an encounter story about Steve J. that is SERIOUSLY unique!

In 1982, I organized a dinner with Steve Jobs & Steve Wozniak at one of the most expensive restaurants in the U.S.: A meticulously elegant place in Boston called L'Espalier. The dinner was in conjunction with Apple fest '82, sponsored by The Boston Computer Society. Our dinner guests included the senior technology reporters of The Wall Street Journal, BusinessWeek and The NY Times.

As we were finishing dessert, Steve suddenly—with no warning—pulled his chair back and stood up in the middle of the restaurant. He began talking loudly to all of the patrons.

I was mortified. Steve was 27 years old and looked like a ruffled hippie. No one in the restaurant would have any idea who this rude young man was. And Steve just didn't get it: This is a Boston establishment and you DON'T do things like this in Boston.

The hushed conversations in the restaurant abruptly stopped.

Steve was telling everyone about **"This Apple fest computer show across the street at the Hynes Convention Centre."**

"And," he said, "...this whole event was organized by THIS GUY, Jonathan!"

Dear God, I thought, he is humiliating me in front of Boston's elite and the business technology press at the same time.

"AND," Steve said next. "Jonathan is only NINETEEN YEARS OLD. Jonathan is single and WE NEED TO FIND HIM A GIRLFRIEND!"

The restaurant went dead silent. And, then, a moment later, a very well dressed couple seated at another table suddenly raises their hands.

"Oh, oh," the husband said. "Our daughter is available!"

The entire restaurant broke out laughing.

Rome Summer[84]

I met Steve Jobs in Rome in the summer of 1985.

When Steve's stop in Rome on the way to the USSR was announced, the news of the turmoil in Cupertino had already reached us Apple concessionaries in Italy. There were about twenty of us by then. We were anxious to know what was really going on in the U.S. headquarters of the company. We were especially worried about our investments on the Macintosh computer promotion and on related inventory.

The day Jobs arrived we were waiting him in our best formal clothes, as we thought adequate for receiving someone who became worth US$ 500 million while still in his twenties.

Finally a dark blue limousine arrived and out came this young man dressed in a rumpled white T-shirt, faded blue jeans and worn basketball shoes. He proceeded straight to the dais mounted near the building, where the worried-looking Apple dignitaries joined him. He tapped the microphone and then sized with a crooked smile the assembled crowd. He said a few perfunctory words about his impending trip to USSR. Then, after a pause, put serious face and addressed the Italian executives standing beside him: "Now I have something to ask you", he said solemnly. A dramatic silence ensued, everybody expecting at least a hint about what was going on in Cupertino. But instead he pointed with his thumb at the palazzina and, again with his crooked smile, he asked, "How much did you pay for this beauty?" A nervous laugh came from all from the audience, and that was the end of the meeting. He climbed down from the dais, chatted lightly for a few minutes with Apple people, shook hands with everybody, back to the limousine and joined his fiancée for a bicycle tour around Tuscany.

Pixar Campus visit[85]

It was me, Van Toffler (president of MTV Networks Music Group), Tom Freston (CEO of MTV-parent company Viacom), and Jimmy Iovine (music producer, chairman of Interscope-Geffen). It was Jimmy who introduced us to Jobs, **and we flew up to Pixar to go meet him**. I'm a product guy, so it was thrilling for me. If you're a product guy, Steve Jobs is the guy you want to meet. He was incredibly gracious and nice.

We had been thinking up ideas about how we could work with Apple...So, I give him my views on the future of music, and I was always big on subscription services. He listened and then he said, "Jason, you seem like a nice guy, but your ideas are all wrong." He was so blunt and funny, the whole room burst into laughter. Later, he takes us on a tour of Pixar and shows us some clips of the movie they're working on, and as we're walking around the beautiful Pixar campus, Freston turns to me and says: "Don't talk in the next meeting." We laughed.

Online distribution Vehicle[86]

2006, Steve Jobs was negotiating with Fox and other studios to expand iTunes from selling digital music and TV shows to selling feature films.

Unfortunately, many of those views were inconsistent with existing media, and as was often the case, he thought the studio guys were Luddites. I was one of them. We spent many hours on the phone and in person hashing out ways to reconcile the new offering with our concerns about it. **We were very eager to make it work** -- but nowhere near as eager as Steve, who wanted to corral all the studios and make one of his bold and exciting announcements, which he'd scheduled for September.

We argued and debated back and forth into the summer, and as August arrived, we remained a fair distance apart. So, as a respite from Relentless Steve, I sneaked off to my annual retreat on the tiny island of Antiparos, near Paros in Greece. I thought I was safe. But not from Steve. He stalked me, eventually sending this e-mail:

From: Steve Jobs
Date: Sat, 26 Aug 2006 16:51:12 -0700
To: Jim Gianopulos
Cc: Steve Jobs
Subject: I'm coming to Paros

Jim,

We need to talk and if that's not possible over the phone or via e-mail, then I need to come to Paros and go for a walk on the beach with you and resolve this. The time is now to begin creating a new online distribution vehicle for movies, and Apple is the company to do it. I need your help.

How do I find you once I get to the airport on Paros?

Thanks.
Steve

He never made it to Paros, but we eventually made a deal, and it evolved into a great friendship, one that I will always cherish.

Washing Dishes[87]

We were in Jobs' neighborhood two weekends ago having dinner with some friends of my parents, and we decided to take a walk in order to look at Steve Jobs' and Steve Young's houses, which are right next to each other. We headed over, and all of a sudden were alongside Jobs house. It's a really unusual and interesting house, but much understated and relatively small. You can just freely walk on the sidewalk right next to it.

Well, we were walking along, and I heard dishes clattering, coming from his house, and I look over and there he was in his kitchen window, black turtleneck and all, **washing dishes**. He just looked up at us, maybe 15 feet away. Nothing in between us but a window, no tall fence (a short, decorative, waist-high one). And we just walked on and proceeded to admire the apple orchard he has in his front yard, and even walked up his driveway a little to see his tulip garden.

His neighbour, who we were walking with, told us that his security lives in the house next door, and he is under constant surveillance, but I still couldn't help but be shocked at how simple and unassuming his house was, and the fact that we saw him washing his dishes.

Hands Shake[88]

I used to work at one of the Apple Stores here in New York. He was scheduled to come in, we didn't know exactly when. He got out of a town car out front, walked in, and right up to me - shaking my hand and saying, **"Hi, I'm Steve Jobs!** Is [name of the store manager] here?"** When I said he was and called him, [Jobs] said he was going to run to the bathroom first - and went to the customer's bathroom (which anyone can use - and isn't exactly the cleanest). He came out, walked right back up to me, and started talking about the store. After about 5 min customers around us starting walking up asking to take pictures, and asking questions, when he promptly asked to be excused and left - back to the car and away.

We had all heard stories about his desire to **not shake hands** (he offered first), his desire to not be in public (he spent his entire time in full view in open areas of the store) and his general shitty attitude (he was super nice and cordial).

Lighted iMacs[89]

It's Monday morning, and Jobs is onstage at the Flint Centre in Cupertino, obsessing. Tomorrow the auditorium will overflow with thousands of Apple loyalists; right now he's rehearsing the killer moment where he says, **"Say hello to the new iMacs,"** and the machines glide out from behind the dark curtain and across the stage. But the current lighting leaves their translucence insufficiently vivid on the gigantic onstage screen. So Jobs wants the lights brighter and turned on earlier in the roll-out. The producer, Steph Adams, speaks into his headset, telling the backstage guys to yeah, just try it again, with the edgy tone of a man whose job consists of placating a perfectionist. No good. Jobs jogs halfway up the aisle and slouches into a centre seat, his legs slung over the seat backs of the next row. **"Let's keep doing it till we get it right, O.K.?"**

They go again. **The iMacs are still under lighted. "No, no,"** Jobs whines, agonized. **"This isn't working at all."**

And again. Now the lights are bright enough, but they're still coming on too late. "I'm getting tired of asking about this," Jobs growls.

Again. And finally they get it right, the five impeccably lighted iMacs gleaming as they glide forward smoothly on the giant screen. "Oh! Right there! That's great!" Jobs yells, elated at the very notion of a universe capable of producing these insanely beautiful machines. "That's perfect!" he bellows, his voice booming across the empty auditorium. "Wooh!"

And you know what? He's right. The iMacs do look better when the lights come on earlier.

Prank E-mails[90]

The San Francisco Chronicle reported that interim CEO Steve Jobs and Apple board member Larry Ellison were apparently so annoyed by a computer consultant who wants to be Apple CEO that they sent prank e-mails telling the executive he had the job. The newspaper reported Wednesday that Jobs and Ellison, who is also chairman and CEO of Oracle Corp., both sent e-mail messages to Michael Murdock, a Burlingame, California-based computer consultant, two days before Christmas, telling him he had the job.

"OK. You can have the job. -- Larry," was one message sent to Murdock, who has been conducting an e-mail campaign for the top job, the Chronicle reported. Jobs reportedly wrote, **"Yep, Mike, it's all yours. When can you start?"** Murdock said he took the messages seriously and said he could start work January 5. The newspaper said Jobs replied, **"Please do not come to Apple."**

Apple Computer spokeswoman Katie Cotton said the situation was **"completely ridiculous"** and said that Jobs had responded to **Murdock "in jest" because of the numerous e-mails he had received.** "This particular person was just firing e-mails and sending e-mails to Steve and Larry on a regular basis and in jest. Steve responded to him," she said. "He has taken it too far," Cotton said, referring to Murdock, who said she has been calling media organizations with the story. But Murdock -- who said he quit his job as a Macintosh Systems engineer at Pixar Animation Studios Inc., where Jobs is also chairman, in August -- said he has not harassed Apple or any of the individuals involved.

Logo[91]

During one of our agency's regularly scheduled marketing meetings with Steve, he asked for our advice on what he felt was a conundrum. Which was more important — **to make the logo look right to the owner before the PowerBook was opened,** or to have it look right to the rest of the world when the machine was in use?

Look around today and the answer is pretty obvious. Every laptop on earth has **a logo that's right-side up when the machine is opened.** Back then, it wasn't so obvious, probably because laptops were not yet ubiquitous.

So we debated the issue. There were decent arguments on both sides. It seemed like we were damned if we did and damned if we didn't. Remember, Steve was the guy who put the customer experience first. In the end, that was the reason he ended making the decision he did. He thought that the most important person in the equation was the one who shelled out good money to buy the product in the first place.

It was only when later PowerBook models were designed that Steve reconsidered and decided the **logo should face the world right-side up.** That one fleeting moment of pleasure for the owner started to feel tiny in comparison. Looking back, it borders on the unbelievable that something so wrong could ever have seemed right. That Steve Jobs ever wrestled with this decision only proves one thing: being right in retrospect is much easier being right in real time.

Argument[92]

The closest thing [Steve Jobs and I] ever had to an argument was when I left in 1985 to start a company to build a universal remote control. I went to [design agency of which Apple was a client] Frog Design to do the design. Steve dropped in there one day and he saw what they were designing for me and he threw it against the wall and said they could not do any work for me. **"Anything you do for Woz, belongs to me."** I was on my own, but I was still friendly with Apple. But Steve had a burst-out there. The people at Frog told me about it. That was the only time there was ever a fight between us, but it wasn't actually between us. **Nobody has ever seen us having an argument.**

Computer[93]

Diane Keaton, 65, says she met Jobs in the late '70s, when the late computer genius was her NYC neighbour. Steve wanted to meet the "Annie Hall" star, so she went over for a visit. But things went downhill fast.

"**[A]ll he's talking about is the computer thing,**" Keaton recalls. "How the computer was going to take over the world. And I'm sitting there like, 'OK, right.' And he keeps talking about how everyone is going to **have a computer in their life**, in their world, in their home. And I'm going, 'Right, And Right.'"

Unfortunately, all the tech talk didn't go over well with the actress, who says she never saw Jobs again. "[B]ecause obviously I just wasn't prepared for that. I thought, 'Is he nuts?'" But Keaton does regret leaving Steve: "Can you imagine? What an idiot I was."

U2 iPod[94]

Steve was trying to sort out one of the fundamental questions of the age: is there any value to a musician's work? He thought that with iTunes, he could make it easier for people who wanted to respect intellectual copyright. So we had the idea to offer "Vertigo" for an iPod commercial, and we went out to see Steve at his house in Palo Alto and he was like, "What? You guys want to give me a song for a commercial? Wow, that's great, that's amazing." Then we said we wanted to be in the commercial, and he said "Maybe, yeah, I don't see why not."

Then we said we don't want to be paid, but we'd **like a U2 iPod,** a black one. His first response was, "That doesn't work at all. IPods are white!" But it turned out lots of people wanted them – and not because of U2. **Because they were red and black!**

My Health⁹⁵

In my own involvement with him, my real personal enjoyment of him as a man, he was a clear thinker, on lots of subjects, and I could turn to him. My actual last conversation with him was he called me **because he was worried about my health, which is a clue to him.** This tough guy was very tender, and he said, **"I don't like the look of you, you look worn out,"** and I said, "What? I'm fine!" He wouldn't listen to me.

When I hurt my spine and I was in trouble, this package arrived of books and CDs and music and honey from their garden – tons of stuff arrived at the house. And so, yes, he was a captain of industry, a warrior for his companies. But I found him to be a very thoughtful friend, and a wonderfully detailed and interested parent of his kids, and lover of his wife.

Install[96]

Today, I met Steve Jobs! It was as simple as "Hello, I'm Steve... nice to meet you. Come on into my house." And with that, we walked through his front gate and through the garage to the backyard.

[...] **We set up in the back corner of the yard, and began the install, which took us three hours to complete.** During the process, he would come out and check on us every 45 minutes or so, usually staying for a bit to chat about the trampoline, the company that built it, the manufacturing process, or how the trampoline could be simplified and improved upon. We didn't really get any opportunities to chat about things outside the task at hand, but it was nice that he would spend any time at all with us. He even got up to test-jump a bit too (I really, really wish I had that on video).

[...] He finally finished talking and came around back. Rob explained a little about the safety rules and the specifics of the install as we walked back towards the back corner of the yard. He jumped up inside the trampoline and started jumping with his daughter. It was really sweet. He jumped around inside a bit, then got out and gave some encouraging words to her and her friends. Then he paid us the install fee (plus the largest tip Rob has ever received on an install).

"And one more thing" we sheepishly said; "Can you sign our iPods???"

"You don't want me to do that — it will rub off," he quips.

He looks at mine and continues, "And that one is going to be a collectors' item soon!" I think to myself, "exactly!" and say "true, it's a classic design."

Turned away[97]

Everyone knows Parisians are snobs. So it probably shouldn't have come as a surprise that an unshaven, middle-aged American, speaking English and dressed in cuffed jeans, sneakers, and a worn black T-shirt, **was rudely turned away from the bar at a lavish fete inside Paris's Musee d'Orsay on September 16, 2003.**

Except that the man was Steven P. Jobs, the cofounder and chief executive of Apple Computer Inc., and it was his party. And some bash it was. For three hours, Apple's guests grazed on foie gras and seared tuna canapés, and sipped champagne while strolling under a massive glass arcade that shelters one of the world's largest collections of Impressionist masters, Rodin sculpture, and art nouveau furniture. In a Baroque salon at the far end of the museum, a raucous jazz band played. As one guest observing the scene intoned, "This is huge."

IMac[98]

Jobs said he was betting the company on the machine and so it needed a great name. He suggested one at the meeting, Segall says, but it was terrible. [It was later revealed the name was 'MacMan']

Jobs said the new computer was a Mac, so the name had to reference the Macintosh brand. The name had to make it clear the machine was designed for the internet. It also had to be applicable to several other upcoming products. And it had to be quick: the packaging needed to be ready in a week.

Segall says he came back with five names. Four were ringers, sacrificial lambs for the name **he loved — iMac.** "It referenced the Mac, and the "I" meant internet," Segall says. "But it also meant individual, imaginative and all the other things it came to stand for." The "I" prefix could also be applied to whatever other internet products Apple was working on. Jobs rejected them all, including iMac.

"He didn't like iMac when he saw it," Segall says. "I personally liked it, so I went back again with three or four new names, **but I said we still like "iMac."** He said: 'I don't hate it this week, but I still don't like it.'"

Segall didn't hear any more about the name from Jobs personally, but friends told him that Jobs was silk-screening the name on prototypes of the new computer. He was testing it out to see if it looked good. "He rejected it twice but then it just appeared on the machine," Segall says, laughing. "He never formally accepted it."

Family screening[99]

The night before our interview, Jobs and his kids sat down for their **first family screening** of Pixar's 2004 release "The Incredible." After that, he tracked the countdown to the 100 millionth song sold on the iTunes store. Apple had promised a prize to the person who moved the odometer to 10 figures, and as the big number approached, fortune seekers snapped up files at a furious rate. At around 10:15, 20-year-old Kevin Britten of Hays, Kans., bought a song by the electronica band Zero 7, and Jobs himself got on the phone to tell him that he'd won. Then Jobs asked a potentially embarrassing question:

"Do you have a Mac or PC?"

"I have a Macintosh... duh!" said Britten.

Jobs laughs while recounting this.

Sign my iPod[100]

As the conversation went: "I hear you're not really one to give autographs, but I just gotta ask....**will you sign my iPod?** Its fine if you don't want to. **I'm not normally one to even ask for autographs"**.

Steve: *chuckling* "it's quite alright. You heard that about me?? Well I wouldn't say that I don't like giving autographs, I guess I was never comfortable with the idea solely taking credit for something, which is to me what an autograph might imply. To be honest, I think I'm the last person who should sign something. A writer signing a book I can understand, but I think if anybody within our company should sign something, it should be members from our R&D team and all the others responsible for product innovation. It's unfortunate that they all can't receive the same level recognition. But I suppose it's easier this way though? You would need a pretty big iPod to fit all those signatures".

Enjoy[101]

In 2007, Mayer was offered an offer he couldn't turn down from RIM who wanted to sponsor his summer tour. Mayer had no reservations about saying yes but decided to give Jobs a call just to give him a quick heads up and let him know that the RIM contract would require him to use RIM products exclusively. Thankfully for him RIM only made smartphones!

So Mayer calls up Jobs who, believe it or not, praises RIM for the work they do and casually mentions that he'll send Mayer an iPhone "to at least play with on the bus."

"I accepted the offer with Blackberry, and in the months leading up to the July 29th release date, the iPhone became the most desired item on the planet. Everybody wanted one, and nobody had yet to see one in person. It was mythical. That day I was playing an amphitheatre in Indianapolis, and sometime in the afternoon the production office got a call over the radio that a sales associate from the local Apple Store was standing at the outermost gate of the venue with something addressed to me. A few minutes later someone knocked on my dressing room door and handed me an Apple Store bag. Inside was an iPhone, and taped to it was a card; it belonged to Steve Jobs, CEO, 1 Infinite Loop, Cupertino, California. Handwritten on the backside of the card was **one word: 'Enjoy!'**"

Bouquet of flowers[102]

Pito showed Steve a clunky, character-based, primitive spreadsheet, but all of the elements of the future were there: there were formulas at the bottom of the spreadsheet, rather than integrated in the cells; it was multi-dimensional; and the user could instantly call up different views of the same data set.

Immediately, Jobs wanted Back Bay for the NeXT. "He kept getting more excited; he was the most excited person in the room," remembers Pito.

Back Bay fit right in with Steve's vision, says Allen: "Right from the start, he was looking for something new... It might have been better financially for his company to get 1-2-3 [ported to the NeXT], but that would have compromised his vision.... [Back Bay] was attractive because it was a new kind of spreadsheet."

A few days after the decision [to port Black Bay to the NeXT platform], Steve Jobs sent a huge **bouquet of flowers to Cambridge.** "It was like he was wooing us," says Lynda. "It must have been three feet tall!"

Called rainy Sunday afternoon[103]

He was a bit of a hero of mine. So I wrote a letter. Sure, email existed at the time, but a letter seemed more real. I wrote about how I grew up with a Mac Plus, about my experience at our alma mater Reed College, and about my hopes for my life. I explained that I knew he wasn't going to give me my magical dream job, or any job for that matter. But I wanted to let him know that he was an example to me of how to live one's life -- to take chances, work hard, and never compromise on yourself. After dropping the letter in the mailbox, I promptly forgot about it, never thinking it would ever get past the gates.

Several months later, **on a rainy Sunday afternoon**, I got a call. It went exactly like this:

"Hello?"

"Hello. May I speak with Lucas Haley?"

"Speaking."

"Hi. This is Steve Jobs."

At this point I was ready to call bull on whichever friend was prank calling me. I barely caught myself in time, remembering that I hadn't told anyone about the letter. This couldn't be anyone but Steve Jobs. The sudden realization strengthened my suspicion that I hadn't said anything in an awkwardly long time, and I blurted out a weak "Can ... **can I help you?"**

Steve Jobs and I spoke on the phone that afternoon for over 20 minutes, about college, about work, about chasing dreams, and about how he couldn't give me a job but here's the name of someone who could. It was all very surreal, and immediately upon hanging up it felt like it couldn't have happened.

Three dot[104]

Steve had no idea who Herb Caen was, much less the tremendous clout he had with hundreds of thousands of Bay Area followers who religiously read his "Baghdad by the Bay" daily columns. One mention in one of Herb's **"three dot"** columns could make or break your social life or even your career. So, I introduced Steve to Herb.

Herb said, "It's a great pleasure to meet you at last," and Steve's only reply was, "how come the Chronicle is such a bad newspaper?"

"It used to be a good paper," Herb said with a twinkle in his eyes. "Why, what would you consider a good newspaper?"

This certainly got Will Hearst attention. "Hopefully, the Examiner," he laughed.

"I only read the San Jose Mercury," Steve said. "It covers the greatest industry in the Universe like no one else."

"But Steve," Will interjected, "The Mercury is in Silicon Valley so of course they cover technology more."

Steve Jobs joke[105]

Just as my vision turned into a painful blur, Steve turned to Andrew and asked, "What makes you think a dull PC guy like yourself can appreciate an elegant machine for artists like the Macintosh?"

"Well, Steve," Andrew chuckled, "I didn't used to be so dull. Before PC World, I edited the Whole Earth Catalogue, **and I'm still a Dead-Head.**"

"Look," I volunteered, "Andrew actually went to the Dead concert in Egypt and we were both at the US Festival–this IBM thing is just something we fell into and gosh, you can't blame us, it's been quite an amazing trip."

"Oh, yeah, and I suppose you both dropped acid on your way to Cupertino this morning?"

We all laughed at Steve's joke.

Magazine[106]

Watching Steve dial the number I gave him, I could feel my heart pounding as I hoped to hell Uncle Pat was high in the sky somewhere over the Pacific on his way to some country like Cambodia where telephone reception wasn't so good. Unlikely as might seem, though, McGovern was once again at his desk.

"You must be a lousy businessman," Jobs began, "You paid $16 million for **Wayne Green's magazines** and yet you want me to pay you to have David and Andrew **produce a magazine for Apple.**"

I couldn't hear everything McGovern said but he was talking loudly enough in an excited voice that I did hear, "don't believe everything you read in the Chronicle."

"You're investing in Micro80 but not Macworld!" Steve shouted back, "Micro80 looks like yesterday leftover oatmeal. If you want to publish Macworld you need to belly up to the bar!"

And then he hung up. I was dumbfounded.

"Don't worry, David," Jobs laughed, **"McGovern will come around and we'll still have a magazine."**

Images for Mac screens[107]

Steve walked in dressed in a beautiful pinstriped, double-breasted suit with a white shirt and red tie. Right away, there was a problem — Steve didn't like the images we had chosen for the Mac screens. Aware that he might bolt any moment, Andrew and I worked feverishly to fix them — putting up exactly what Steve said he wanted. Meanwhile he stared at Mosgrove, and said, "Are you one of those type of photographers who takes dozens of photos hoping one of them will turn out okay?" Will just looked at him and shrugged.

"Take a picture of this," Steve said, holding up his middle finger. We stared in disbelief. Someone must have keyed his Mercedes again, I remember thinking.

Crazy as it was, the "computer gods" were with us that day. Somehow we got our Steve Jobs photo and it is a classic, but if I wasn't a nimble thinker it would never have appeared. **A couple weeks after the photo shoot, Steve called to say, "Gee, David, I've changed my mind, I don't want to be on the cover of Macworld."**

"Too late," I lied, "the cover is already at the printer and we can't change it."

In reality, a few pages were at the printer, but not the cover, and we could have changed it if we really wanted to, which, of course, we didn't.

Backyard Pool Party[108]

Here in Palo Alto, Steve Jobs isn't just an icon, he's also the guy who lives down the street. I first met Steve years ago at a backyard pool party.

The next time I met him was when our children attended school together. He sat in on back-to-school night listening to the teacher drone on about the value of education while the rest of us sat around pretending having Steve Jobs in the room was totally normal.

[...] It was at Halloween not long after when I realized he actually knew my name. He and his wife put on a darn scary haunted house [...]. He was sitting on the walkway, dressed like Frankenstein. As I walked by with my son, Steve smiled and said, "Hi Listen." My son thought I was the coolest mom in town when he realized The Steve Jobs knew me. Thanks for the coolness points, Steve.

In time, things changed. The walks were less frequent, the gait slower, the smile not so ready. Earlier this year when I saw Steve and his wife walking down our street holding hands.

While Newsweek and the Wall Street Journal and CNET continue to drone on about the impact of the Steve Jobs era, I won't be pondering the MacBook Air I write on or the iPhone I talk on. I will think of the day I saw him at his son's high school graduation. There Steve stood, tears streaming down his cheeks, his smile wide and proud, as his son received his diploma and walked on into his own bright future leaving behind a good man and a good father who can be sure of the rightness of this, perhaps his most important legacy of all.

Beer-and-food event at Apple[109]

Steve J. gave a beer-and-food event at Apple today to celebrate the new Chiat-Day ad campaign. As part of his praise for the new ad and its theme, "Think Different", he read a letter written by the mother of a child that was "different" regarding her child's response to the ad. It was a really lovely letter - brought tears to my eyes. If you can, you should get a copy of the letter and post it. The letter was initially sent to someone at Chiat-Day.

Steve said that the feedback on the ad was about 75% favourable. The other 25% of negative reactions to the ad had that "come on, let's show 'em why we kick Microsoft's butt!" flavour. Steve said that back when we DID kick Microsoft butt by about a factor of 100, this was easy to do. Only took 15...30...maybe 60 seconds at the most to convey that message. Now that we only kick Microsoft's butt by a factor of 2, this is not a good strategy because it's much harder to convince people of that difference that quickly. Rather, we should adopt the techniques of someone like Nike.

He quoted some figures. Apple spends 100 million $ a year on advertising. And it hasn't done us much good, Steve admitted. We'll continue to spend the same amount. Not much more or less. Only we'll spend it better. Because [...] our brand is the most - or at least one of the most - valuable things we have going for us now. Then he read the letter I mentioned earlier. It was a good - no, great - speech, delivered in an "I may sound like I'm musing but I'm damned sure of what I'm saying" tone.

And the beer did not suck!

The clip[110]

On the stage of the auditorium that would hold the event, Jobs stood back and watched as his television production crew screened a video to be shown after he introduced the iMac. Marketing mini-documentaries were commonplace in the tech business: lots of product shots from flattering angles, edgy Greek chorus-like close-ups of talking-head executives and industry analysts singing the praises of the new product. Jobs watched with an eagle eye as the sharply edited vignettes ran on the large screen. One of the highlights was a playful reference to the retro-futuristic look of the egg-shaped, lollipop blue machine, which looked like something from the 1960s animated television series The Jetsons. As homage, **the video included a five-second clip from the actual series.**

Then one of the production guys gingerly approached Jobs and warned him of a problem. It seemed that Hanna-Barbera, the animation house that owned the rights to the Jetsons, had yet to sign off. The permission was still stalled with the lawyers. If the issue isn't resolved before tomorrow, the nervous media specialist told Jobs, the clip will have to go.

Jobs' face turned to steel. "Keep it in," he said.

"Ummmmm, Steve, we can't do that," said the production guy. He began to explain what Jobs certainly knew from his other job as majority shareholder of the Pixar studio and thereby the owner of some of the animation world's most valuable intellectual property: **using the clip without permission could incur huge liabilities. Jobs abruptly cut him off. "I don't care!" he shouted. "We're using it."**

The clip stayed in the picture. And the iMac, a beneficiary of that perfectionism, did indeed initiate a string of Apple products that made the company one of the most admired corporations on the face of the earth.

Fantastic[111]

At the end of this presentation, Jobs pulled back a sheet that had covered an elliptical object on the conference table. The first new product on his grid: the iMac. It was a weird, egg-shaped beast but disarmingly attractive. Like all great Steve Jobs products, it had a human feel to it. You wanted to touch it. Its plastic case was a feel-good shade of fruity blue. During its development the informal code names for the project had been the names of Columbus's ships: Nina, Pinta, and Santa Maria. Why? "A new world," he explained.

After putting the machine through its paces, he bore down on me. "Isn't that just great?" he asked, with the pride of a very pushy parent. Yes, I agreed, it's really neat. "It's not just 'neat'," he corrected me. "**It's fucking fantastic**."

Music¹¹²

Jobs had always been unapologetic about the incompatibility [between iPod and **other music software** than iTunes], insisting that Apple should not make iPods interoperable with competitors until its customer demand it. I once tried to get him to admit that the limitation was unfriendly to customers, but he would not bulge. He challenged me to provide an example where Apple's actions could harm a listener. Finally I came up with something.

"You love Bob Dylan, Steve," I said. "He records with Sony, your competitor in selling music. What if Sony sold a really great, previously unreleased Dylan song on its music store? None of your iTunes customers could download it and listen to it on their computers or iPods. Isn't that a disadvantage?"

"Bob Dylan loves us," said Jobs. "He's never do that?"

I thought that was a fairly lame comeback. But a few months later, Dylan did okay the release of **two fantastic outtakes from the legendary Blood on the Tracks sessions for online sale —on the iTunes store, not his own label Sony's store.**

Company wide e-mail[113]

On January 13, 2006, something interesting came to Jobs' attention. At Wall Street's close on that Friday afternoon, Apple's market capitalization had reached $72.13 billion. What made it a milestone to Jobs was that the cap of Dell computers at that moment was $71.97 billion — almost a million dollars less.

Recalling Dell's advice almost a decade earlier, **the Apple CEO was moved to send out a companywide e-mail. "Team," he wrote his employees,** "it turned out that Michael Dell wasn't perfect at predicting the future."

Changes the Rules[114]

Jobs has instituted a periodic meeting of what he calls the Apple 100. Ever the elitist, he describes those invited as not the highest-ranking executives on the organizational charts but the really key people, the people, he says, who you'd take on the life raft with you when the ship was sinking (presumably everyone else would go down in the drink). "I usually get up in the beginning," Jobs says, "and say something like 'Our revenues have doubled in the last two years. And our stock price is high and our shareholders are happy. And a lot of people think it's really great, we've got a lot to lose, let's play it safe. That's the most dangerous thing we can do. We have to get bolder, because we have world-class competitors now and we just can't stand still'."

Then Steve Jobs told the hundred what he intended to do. Even though Apple had created one of the most successful consumer electronic products in history and the most popular of those was the tiny iPod mini, he was going to pull the plug on it and make something better. "We are going to redefine the whole industry," he told his people. "By coming up with a player that's a full-featured iPod, colour display, a click wheel, dock connector, photos, everything — **at a size that completely changes the rules.**"

Classic Steve Jobs[115]

I went over to shake [Steve Jobs]'s hand and apologize for the mix-up [relative to Engaged posting an incorrect story about an iPhone delay].

His reaction completely threw me. I expected some of the chiding he was infamous for giving journalists, but I heard not even a hint of frustration. Actually, he just acted as though he had no idea what I was talking about. Like it had never happened. Seriously. This was probably the most unexpected reaction I could have possibly imagined -- **I was completely flummoxed. Of course, I realized moments later he was snowing me big time, and that it was classic Steve passive-aggressive. But you're Steve Jobs, and its lunch time, and what happened, so what exactly DO you say to that whole thing, right?**

Well, my nemesis (and one of my best pals) Brian Lam notices Steve and I interacting, so he rolls over to say hello as well. No sooner than Brian introduces himself, Steve is telling him all about how Gizmodo is his favourite tech blog, and how it's the first site he reads and that he put it above Engaged (motioning upwards with his finger). Ouch.

No Boss[116]

When Steve tried to hire me I said, "I don't like having a boss."

He said, **"A lot of people say working for me is like not having a boss."**

Yes, it's a true story.

Quotes[117]

When the book was finished, Steve asked for a pre-release copy, which I duly sent.

At the time, all sorts of people were telling me **that I needed to put quotes on the back cover of the book.** So I asked Steve Jobs if he'd give me one. Various questions came back. But eventually Steve said, "Isaac Newton didn't have back-cover quotes; why do you want them?"

And that's how, at the last minute, the back cover of A New Kind of Science ended up with just a simple and elegant array of pictures. Another contribution from Steve Jobs that I notice every time I look at my big book.

Freakiest Scenario[118]

Sometime later, I worked on a Twitter client with my pal Buzz. A friend of his who worked at Apple told us this little story.

One day while riding the elevator at Infinite Loop, he found himself in the **freakiest scenario any Apple employee can imagine: alone, with the elevator door opening to let Steve in.** Being a well-adjusted individual, Buzz's friend promptly disappeared into the tap-world of his iPhone, lest he say or do something wrong in Steve's presence. It was still the early days of iPhone apps, and Steve did something that had apparently become a habit with him. He reached for the iPhone and asked,
"What app is that?"
"Birdfeed", came the reply.

Steve tapped here and there, flicked the scroll view a bit, and then handed the phone back. "The background needs more texture," he said.

I'll do better next time, Steve.

Sashimi soba[119]

Jobs was a fruitarian (someone who only eats fruit), and he continued to be a strict vegan throughout his life. But he made an exception for Japanese food.

Such was his love of soba that he sent the chef from Café Mac, **the Apple company cafeteria, to study at the Tsukiji Soba Academy and had him serve a dish called "sashimi soba,"** an original Steve Jobs creation.

Design[120]

Within a couple of minutes, after some quick introductions, everyone settled around big square table, Jobs at one corner, flanked by Dean and Doerr.

"Good morning to everyone," said Tim, "Before we start, we'd like to ask you to hold your questions until after each presentation."
"Yeah, right!" snorted Bezos, followed by that honking laugh.
"Otherwise we might as well not be here," said Jobs.
"How long is your presentation?" asked Doerr. "Each pitch is about ten minutes."
"I can't do that," said Jobs. "I'm not built that way. So if you want me to leave, I will, but I can't just sit here."

Tim studied Jobs , then turned to the screen and put up a spec sheet about Metro and Pro. "As you can see—" began Tim.
"Let's talk about the bigger question," interrupted Jobs. "Why two machines?"
"We've talked about that," said Tim, "and we think—"

"Because I see big problem here," said Jobs.

[...] **What does everyone think about the design?"** asked Doerr, switching subjects.
"What do you think?" said Jobs to Tim. It was a challenge, not a question.
"I think it's coming along," said Tim, "though we expect—" "I think it sucks!" said Jobs.
His vehemence made Tim pause. "Why?" he asked, a bit stiffly.

"It just does."
"In what sense?" said Tim, getting his feet back under him? "Give me a clue."
"Its shape not innovative, it's not elegant, it doesn't feel anthropomorphic," said Jobs, ticking off three of his design mantras.

"You have this incredibly innovative machine but it looks very traditional**." The last word delivered like a stab. [...] "There are design firms out there that could come up with things we've never thought of," Jobs continued, "things that would make you shit in your pants."**

Steve Jobs meet Obama[121]

Jobs, who was known for his prickly, stubborn personality, almost missed meeting President Obama in the fall of 2010 because he insisted that the president personally ask him for a meeting. Though his wife told him that Obama "was really psyched to meet with you," Jobs insisted on the personal invitation, and the standoff lasted for five days. **When he finally relented and they met at the Westin San Francisco Airport, Jobs was characteristically blunt. He seemed to have transformed from a liberal into a conservative.**

"You're headed for a one-term presidency," he told Obama at the start of their meeting, insisting that the administration needed to be more business-friendly. As an example, Jobs described the ease with which companies can build factories in China compared to the United States, where "regulations and unnecessary costs" make it difficult for them. Jobs also criticized America's education system, saying it was "crippled by union work rules," noted Isaacson. "Until the teachers' unions were broken, there was almost no hope for education reform." Jobs proposed allowing principals to hire and fire teachers based on merit, that schools stay open until 6 p.m. and that they be open 11 months a year.

Jobs suggested that Obama meet six or seven other CEOs who could express the needs of innovative businesses -- but when White House aides added more names to the list, Jobs insisted that it was growing too big and that "he had no intention of coming." In preparation for the dinner, Jobs exhibited his notorious attention to detail, telling venture capitalist John Doerr that the menu of shrimp, cod and lentil salad was "far too fancy" and objecting to a chocolate truffle dessert. But he was overruled by the White House, which cited the president's fondness for cream pie.

New baby[122]

At a high-school gym in Berkeley, Calif., [Steve Jobs is] rehearsing the rollout that will introduce his new baby, the NeXT computer, to the world. Dressed in blue jeans and a red flannel shirt, Jobs paces back and forth, reading lines into a wireless microphone. [...]. When the first slide appears on the screen, Jobs enthuses: "I really like that green." Around him, other NeXT executives chime in: "Great green. Great green".

The computer goes through its paces, playing music with the sound of a live orchestra, pulling up images as clear as photographs, retrieving quotes from a memory bank big enough to hold a bookshelf full of classics. Then a software glitch makes the image on the sleek black monitor freeze. NeXT employees tense up, expecting an infamous Jobs outburst. Jobs just stares at the screen, then shrugs. "We're hosed," he says calmly. "We'll fix that. No problem."

Later, a video shows the automated assembly plant that Jobs has built to manufacture the NeXT machines. Wandering back to sit with a handful of employees, Jobs watches as robot hands install the state-of-the-art chips that will power the computer. For a second he looks almost teary. "It's beautiful," he says softly.

Brightest and Sharpest[123]

Jobs could be ruthless when he talked to the labels. Kevin Gage, then Warner's technology vice president, remembers one key meeting at Apple's Cupertino, California headquarters where he and Vidich tried to persuade Jobs that digital rights management - virtual "locks" to prevent songs from being shared - was necessary to get other labels on board.

He was three slides into a PowerPoint presentation when Jobs, rocking in his chair, exploded into a tirade about how the music business just didn't get it. "He said, 'You've got your head stuck up your ass' to me a number of times," Gage recalls. "There's that side of Steve - but in a smooth kind of way. He never reacted to Roger [Ames, then Warner's CEO] the same way he reacted to Paul and myself, put it that way. When Roger came into the room, **you saw Steve at his brightest and sharpest.**"

Hip-Hop music[124]

No matter how influential he became, Jobs was still a Beatles fan.

Former Apple executive Tony Fadell, who worked closely with Jobs as senior vice president of the iPod division, remembers a lunch when Jobs received a phone call from Paul McCartney and excitedly declared, "Oh my God! I gotta take this!"

Jobs was open to new music, but his favorite artists were the ones he got to know when he came of age in the Sixties, including Bob Dylan and Donovan. After one meeting with Inters cope chair Jimmy Iovine, he returned to work and asked colleagues, **"Did you know there's this really great thing called hip-hop music?"**

"This was, like, 2004!" Fadell recalls fondly. "We all turned to each other and smiled."

Apple Comeback[125]

"Apple has already come back," and now that his days are not so intently involved in crisis management, and he is able to spend more time with his family, he appears to be having a wonderful time.

He runs Apple in a mode that can only be described as post-CEO. Sometimes he will greet visitors in shorts, sandals and a two-day beard growth. His office is a surprisingly compact rectangle cluttered with books, videos and advertising awards. On the phone, sitting at a desk that sports both Mac and Windows laptops [running NeXT STEP], he schmoozes and deals with everyone from Pixar executives to Jerry Seinfeld, concerning Apple's ad on the Final Episode.

Last week he spent an extraordinary amount of time monitoring every last detail of the iMac intro; a typical executive decision was the elimination of a clarinet on a video soundtrack because it sounded "too synthetic."

Leakiest organization[126]

One of the struggles we were going through when he came back was that Apple was about the leakiest organization in history — it had gotten so bad that people were cavalier about it. In the face of all those leaks, I remember the first all company e-mail that Steve sent around after becoming Interim CEO again — he talked in it about how Apple would release a few things in the coming week, and a desire to tighten up communications so that employees would know more about what was going on — and how that required more respect for confidentiality. **That mail was sent on a Thursday; I remember all of us getting to work on Monday morning and reading mail from Fred Anderson, our then-CFO, who said basically: "Steve sent mail last week, he told you not to leak, we were tracking everyone's mail, and 4 people sent the details to outsiders.** They've all been terminated and are no longer with the company."

Well. If it wasn't clear before that the Amelio/Spindler/Sculley days of Apple were over, it was crystal clear then, and good riddance.

Journalists tested iPhone before its release[127]

I was among the few journalists who got to test [the iPhone] before its release. Soon after I received the unit, I was walking down Broadway and my test unit got a call from "Unknown." It was Jobs, ostensibly wanting to know what I thought, but actually making sure I understood how amazing it was. I acknowledged that it was extraordinary, but mentioned to him that maybe nothing could match the expectations he had generated. People were calling it the "Jesus phone." Didn't that worry him? The answer was no. "We are going to blow away the expectations," he told me.

Living legend[128]

My company ASTRO Studios started in downtown Palo Alto in the mid 90's where we shared a small private parking lot with Steve and his private office. In fact, our office windows faced each other on this narrow tree-lined street.

[...] But the thing I remember most often was seeing Steve looking out the back window of this office where he had set up a little gym, his head bobbing up and down as he climbed the stair master. Our young design team could look out from our front window to see this icon of the valley sweating, swigging water and towelling his red face...just like the rest of us. **It gave me a sense that he's not just a living legend, but also a regular guy with a lot of dreams that come true one step at a time.**

Nike+ [129]

We had worked together on a Nike-Apple collaboration called Nike+.
So we took what Apple knows and Nike knows, and brought new technology to
the market. Anyway, long story short, he said, "Congratulations. It's great [that
you've been named CEO]. You're going to do a great job." I said, "Well, do you
have any advice?"

He said, "No, no, you're great." Then there was a pause. "Well, I do have some
advice," he said. "Nike makes some of the best products in the world--products
that you lust after, absolutely beautiful stunning products. But you also make a
lot of crap."

He said, "Just get rid of the crappy stuff, and focus on the good stuff." And then
I expected a little pause and a laugh. But there was a pause, and no laugh at
the end.

Dumbest phone idea[130]

The story goes that ESPN president George Bodenheimer [...] spotted Apple CEO Steve Jobs in a hallway. It seemed like a good time to introduce himself. "I am George Bodenheimer," he said to Jobs. **"I run ESPN." Jobs just looked at him and said nothing other than "Your phone is the dumbest fucking idea I have ever heard," then turned and walked away.**

Think Different[131]

Jobs was quiet during the pitch [of the Think Different campaign by TBWA], but he seemed intrigued throughout, and now it was time for him to talk.

He looked around the room filled with the **"Think Different"** billboards and said, "This is great, this is really great ... but I can't do this. People already think I'm an egotist, and putting the Apple logo up there with all these geniuses will get me skewered by the press."

The room was totally silent. The "Think Different" campaign was the only campaign we had in our bag of tricks, and I thought for certain we were toast.

Steve then paused and looked around the room and said out loud, yet almost as if to his own self, "What am I doing? Screw it. It's the right thing. It's great. Let's talk tomorrow." In a matter of seconds, right before our very eyes, he had done a complete about-face.

Nuclear warfare[132]

The Western Electronic Manufacturers Association used to hold annual industry conferences in Monterey. Steve keynoted one of the conferences in the early 1980s. But rather than tout the greatness of Apple, or the potential of personal computers, or anything material or mundane, **Steve spoke passionately for 40 minutes on one subject -- the dangers of nuclear warfare. That was it.**

The audience, needless to say, was dumbfounded. Steve spoke, took no questions, and sat down. Steve, it turns out, had a lot of passions.

Slides[133]

To my knowledge, the only tech conference Steve Jobs regularly appeared at, the only event he didn't somehow control, was our D: All Things Digital conference, where he appeared repeatedly for unrehearsed, onstage interviews. We had one rule that really bothered him: We never allowed slides, which were his main presentation tool.

One year, about an hour before his appearance, I was informed that he was backstage preparing **dozens of slides,** even though I had reminded him a week earlier of the no-slides policy. I asked two of his top aides to tell him he couldn't use the slides, but they each said they couldn't do it, that I had to. **So, I went backstage and told him the slides were out. Famously prickly, he could have stormed out, refused to go on. And he did try to argue with me. But, when I insisted, he just said "Okay." And he went on stage without them, and was, as usual, the audience's favourite speaker.**

Joint session[134]

For our fifth D conference, both Steve and his long-time rival, the brilliant Bill Gates, surprisingly agreed to a joint appearance, their first extended onstage joint interview ever. But it almost got derailed.

Earlier in the day, before Gates arrived, I did a solo onstage interview with Jobs, and asked him what it was like to be a major Windows developer, since Apple's iTunes program was by then installed on hundreds of millions of Windows PCs. He quipped: **"It's like giving a glass of ice water to someone in Hell."**

When Gates later arrived and heard about the comment, he was, naturally, enraged, because my partner Kara Swisher and I had assured both men that we hoped to keep the joint session on a high plane.

In a pre-interview meeting, **Gates said to Jobs: "So I guess I'm the representative from Hell." Jobs merely handed Gates a cold bottle of water he was carrying.** The tension was broken, and the interview was a triumph, with both men acting like statesmen. When it was over, the audience rose in a standing ovation, some of them in tears.

First retail store[135]

Apple opened its first retail store [...] in the Washington, D.C., suburbs, near my home. [Steve Jobs] conducted a press tour for journalists, as proud of the store as a father is of his first child. I commented that, surely, there'd only be a few stores, and asked what Apple knew about retailing.

He looked at me like I was crazy, said there'd be many, many stores, and that the company had spent a year tweaking the layout of the stores, using a mock-up at a secret location. I teased him by asking if he, personally, despite his hard duties as CEO, had approved tiny details like the translucency of the glass and the colour of the wood.

He said he had, of course.

Frail condition Park visit[136]

After his liver transplant, while he was recuperating at home in Palo Alto, California, Steve invited me over to catch up on industry events that had transpired during his illness. **It turned into a three-hour visit, punctuated by a walk to a nearby park that he insisted we take, despite my nervousness about his frail condition.**

He explained that he walked each day, and that each day he set a farther goal for himself, and that, today, the neighbourhood park was his goal. As we were walking and talking, he suddenly stopped, not looking well. I begged him to return to the house, noting that I didn't know CPR and could visualize the headline: **"Helpless Reporter Lets Steve Jobs Die on the Sidewalk."**

But he laughed, and refused, and, after a pause, kept heading for the park. We sat on a bench there, talking about life, our families, and our respective illnesses (I had had a heart attack some years earlier). He lectured me about staying healthy. And then we walked back.

Cabel with Steve Jobs[137]

Mere hours after iTunes was introduced to the world, with our official meeting at Apple campus only days away, Steven Frank and I were browsing the show floor. "Hey, look, there's Jobs," Steve said while pointing to a large, amoeba-like blob of shuffling black t-shirts. "Oh, man... I gotta talk to him," I declared. I have no idea why — it was like I was being pushed an unseen force. Mind you, I'm a person that loves to talk to people, but even I don't generally go rushing into things like, you know, trying to talk to the CEO of Apple in the middle of madness. But, talk I did, making my way into the show-floor throng and anxiously saying hello.

We talked briefly and, looking back, it was rather fun.

"Hi Steve, its Cabel, from Panic."
"Oh, hey Cabel! Nice to meet you. So tell me, what'd you think of iTunes?"

"Well, I think it looks great! You guys have done a great job with it. But, you know, I still feel we'll do all-right with Audion."
"Oh, really? That's interesting, because honestly? I don't think you guys have a chance."

Ah ha! Some of that famous Jobs magic I'd heard about! Fortunately, it came across more like a teasing jab than a cruel stab — to be honest, I rather enjoyed his honesty, and it got me in a weird sort of "I'm ready to step to that, girlfriend!" mood.

"Well, Steve, I really think it'll still find an audience," I replied. "We've got a lot of higher-end features that you guys probably won't ever add."
"Yeah? Like what?"

"Well, umm..." I was a bit stumped. "You can keep a count of how many times you've played a song, or you can even rate your songs by popularity..."

Apple boardroom¹³⁸

Anyway, a few moments later, Steve Jobs himself entered the giant Apple boardroom, threw his feet up on the table, and got to the meat of the matter.

[...] Jobs wanted to know how big we were, and how long we've been doing this. He wanted to know a few more things that I can't even really remember. I remember he asked, "Do you have any other ideas for apps you want to work on?" I replied, genuinely, "Well, we've got an idea for a digital photo management program..." and he replied with a simple, "Yeah. Don't do that one." Everyone in the room laughed but I had no idea why — remember, my head was still exploding — so Steven Frank had to explain to me that he meant, basically, it was already being made and, of course, it would be called iPhoto. Oh. I get it now.

We also seem to remember Jobs painted us a vibrant (but genuinely honest) picture of how he viewed Audion fairing against iTunes: "It's like you guys are a little push-cart going down the railroad tracks, and we're a giant steam engine about to run you down."

[...] Anyway, when it came time to conclude the point of the meeting, Jobs summed everything up in a very persuasive and powerful way: "We want you guys to work with us. You guys have shown us that you can do a lot with a little. You guys kick ass. Your software totally kicks ass. Cabel, your marketing kicks ass. We think you do incredible work and we'd love to have you join us."

English cottage garden[139]

Oh, to have been a fly or two on the wall of the restaurant where, in 1996, Steve Jobs and Penelope Hob house discussed her design for his garden. "He swept into the ... restaurant on his roller blades and sat down," she wrote. "I wish I had taped the conversation. ... I do recall the intensity of his beliefs."

Hob house was preparing for a three-week tour of the United States when she got an unexpected phone call from the Apple co-founder. **"The man just said his name and that he'd like me to come and redesign his garden in Palo Alto, California," she wrote.**

[...] "Mr Jobs asked me to do an English cottage garden," she recalled - a perfect fit for his Tudor-style home on Waverley Street. "That was quite easy for me to do; the plants weren't a problem. It was a really nice project. He didn't know a lot about gardening but he knew the style he wanted. Later, we sent him pictures of every single plant we recommended.

"I was a great admirer of his, and appreciate his ideas about beauty and simplicity," Hob house continued. "He was rather wonderful. He didn't allow other people to have second-rate standards." In three days, she saw no hint of the Jobs that some associates described as "intimidating, demanding, ferocious, arrogant, intolerant, sometimes abusive, and always obsessive about control." With her, he was "a nice courteous man."

Pretty incredible[140]

Three weeks after we launched I got a call in the office from someone at Apple that said, "Scott Forstall wants to talk to you and he's the head software guy." And I said sure...

Only it wasn't Scott that called it was Steve. And Steve never announces where he's gonna be and what he's gonna do because there's too much commotion around it. So he said, "Dag, this is Steve Jobs."

And he wanted me to come over to his house the next day, and I did, and I spent 3 hours with him in front of his fireplace having this surreal conversation about the future. And, you know, he talked about why Apple was going to win, and we talked about how Siri was doing. And he was very excited about the fact that. You know, he was very interested in this area in general but, you know, they're patient, they don't jump on anything until they feel they can go after something new and he felt that we cracked it. So that was his attraction.

I ended up very lucky, timing wise. I got to work with him for a year before he got real sick. **And he's pretty incredible.** The stories are true. All of the stories.

Word Mac[141]

We filled walls and did all sorts of stuff. It needed to have the **word Mac in the name.** And there's an easy way to get on the Internet. When we went in to show Steve there was such things as MacRocket, another was Macster and MacMan. What Steve liked about MacMan was, we thought it sounded a little like Walkman, and he said Sony is a great consumer electronics company, and if there is a run-off from that I don't think it would be a terrible thing. Ten years later Steve wouldn't feel that way any longer.

The thing he told us to keep in mind was because it looked kind of toy like, I don't want it to sound like a toy. Then we all scratched our heads and said MacMan sounds like PacMan, it sounds like a game. But Steve had that "I like it" thing going on and he followed his heart a lot of the time. The only good thing we could do is go back and find a better one. So I came up with five names, I saved the best one for last. And I said, iMac, and we can list bullet points:

* I for Internet
* I for imagination
* I for individual

Steve's reaction? "Hate it." So we come back a week later with three new names, and, "Hate it, hate it, hate it."

But we said we still like this one, iMac. And Steve said.

The next day Steve had it silk-screened on a computer model and he was showing it to his inner circle. There was never a phone call from Steve saying, you guys really are geniuses. It was just silence, and it was suddenly iMac, which was great.

NeXT name Invention[142]

A good friend of mine, Tom Suiter, was a very good friend of Steve's. [...] Steve called him one day when he was starting NeXT — he had broken away from Apple and taken his people, and they were looking for a name for the company. He called him excitedly to say: "Hey Tom, I have this name I'm thinking of for my new company. I'm thinking of calling it Two."

Tom paused and said: "Well, I don't know about that, Steve. People might ask you about what happened to One."

Then Steve said, "That's why I'm calling you. I think it's a good name, but if you've got a better one that'd be great, could you think about that?"

Later Tom found himself listening to a speech from Bill Gates. During the speech Bill Gates kept using the word "next" when he was talking about new technologies coming from Microsoft. He used the word often enough that Tom noted his repetition and thought, "Wait a minute: next, that means future, that's a cool thing." **And the next day he called Steve and said, "I've got the name for you. Next."** And there's that pause on the other end, where with Steve you never know what's going to come. It could be, "That's the stupidest thing I've ever heard," or it could be, "Great." And he says, "I love it!"

Time capsule[143]

Apparently, Jobs was asked to contribute an item to a time capsule that was being created in honour of the theme of that conference: **"The Future Isn't What It Used to be"** (note: in Aspen in 1983). He looked around to find something to add:

After Steve Jobs' speech, in which he used an Apple Lisa computer to control what Celuch recalls was a 6 projector setup, John approached Jobs and asked for something that he could include in the time capsule.

Jobs thought about it for a few seconds and then unplugged the mouse from the Lisa. Celuch recalls that he was amused by the manner in which he was handed the mouse, as Jobs held the mouse by its cord, almost as one would hold a real mouse by the tail. So into the time capsule the Lisa mouse went, where it was buried at the end of the conference to be unearthed about 20 years later.

But that time capsule was never dug up and its location is now a mystery. The land changed hands, improvements were made and the capsule was lost.

Print advertising strategy[144]

According to one person who attended an executive committee meeting soon after the Next acquisition, **one item on the agenda was to discuss print advertising strategy for the then-newly released Macintosh 3400 and Power Mac machines.** Amelio turned the meeting over to the company's vice president of advertising and brand communications, David Roman, who would unveil the "We're Back" series of ads, and urged the group to save their questions until after Roman was finished.

Roman had barely started when Jobs interrupted, clearly agitated. It was apparently something Roman said about placing Macintosh ads in newspapers. "Why do we want to spend all this money on newspaper advertising when these newspapers are killing us on the editorial page?" Jobs asked, as quoted by the person who attended the meeting. [...]

"We were kind of stunned at how quickly Gil lost control of the meeting, about how he was unwilling to stand up to Jobs," said another Apple executive who also attended the meeting. [...] In the end, Amelio's cautious and non-confrontational style created an environment in which Jobs could freely impose his hyper-formidable will.

Conference room[145]

Since Amelio was forced to resign, Jobs has been a regular presence around Apple, patrolling the hallways and pop-quizzing employees on their work. And he has quickly added to his temperamental legend.

According to a person briefed about a recent meeting with Jobs, **Jobs looked around the conference room, remarked that he "always hated this conference room,"** and moved the meeting to a new room. There, he grilled everyone in attendance about his or her role: When one person identified himself as a speech writer, Jobs shook his head, said, "No speech writer," and banished him from the meeting.

Let's hide our Porsches[146]

Software engineer Randy Adams initially turned down Steve Jobs' offer to work at NeXT, the computer company started by Jobs after his ouster from Apple. It was 1985. Adams wasn't ready to go back to work after selling his pioneering desktop software publishing company. Within a few days Jobs was on Adams' answering machine. "You're blowing it, Randy. This is the opportunity of a lifetime, and you're blowing it." Adams reconsidered.

Adams, using some of the cash he'd earned from the sale of his company, bought a Porsche 911 at the same time Jobs did. To avoid car-door dings, they parked near each other–taking up three parking spaces between them. **One day Jobs rushed over to Adams' cubicle and told him they had to move the cars.**

"I said, 'Why?' and he said, 'Randy, we have to hide the Porsches. **Ross Perot is coming by and thinking of investing in the company, and we don't want him to think we have a lot of money.'"** They moved the cars around to the back of NeXT's offices in Palo Alto, Calif. and Perot invested $20 million in the company in 1987 and took a seat on the board.**

$100 bills[147]

[...] Jobs convinced Adams to start a software business around NeXT, which he did with a $2 million investment from Sequoia Capital. But as the business was under way, Jobs called Adams again to let him know that NeXT was going to give up its workstation business and focus instead on software.

"He told me that the cost of hardware is coming down and we think it's a commodity. I said, 'Then why don't you sell PCs?' Jobs told me, 'I'd rather sell dog s— than PCs.'"

Adams says he has many memories of Jobs from those days at NeXT – how Jobs, a vegan, would pass by engineers enjoying their Subway sandwiches and comment, "Oh, the smell of burnt animal flesh. How delightful." **In 1986, Jobs dressed up as Santa Claus and handed out $100 bills to employees.** Adams also said Jobs was constantly telling employees who had screwed up or done something he didn't like to "fire yourself." Was Jobs serious? "Well, if you didn't get a termination notice then you knew he was only kidding."

Typing directly on the screen[148]

In the fall of 2006, my wife, Laura, and I went out to dinner with Steve and his brilliant and lovely wife, Laurene. Sitting outside of the restaurant on California Avenue in Palo Alto waiting for a table to open up, on a balmy Silicon Valley evening, Steve pulled his personal prototype iPhone out of his jeans pocket and said, 'Here, let me show you something.' He took me on a tour through all of the features and capabilities of the new device.

After an appropriate amount of oohing and aahing, I ventured a comment. BlackBerry aficionado as I was, **I said, 'Boy, Steve, don't you think it's going to be a problem not having a physical keyboard? Are people really going to be okay typing directly on the screen?'** He looked me **right in the eye with that piercing gaze and said, 'They'll get used to it.'**

Strength[149]

"Steve was the first guy I found who would be regularly curled up under his desk in the morning after an all-nighter. A lot of people think that success is luck and being in the right place at the right time. But I think if you're willing to work harder than anybody else, you can create an awful lot of your own luck. We tended to have this philosophical relationship. He liked to talk about big ideas and where did big ideas come from. He was always interested in talking about creating products and how do you know when a product is ready for market."

In the early 1980s Bushnell bought a 15,000-square-foot house in Paris and invited all his Silicon Valley friends to a housewarming party. There was a band, lots of food and drink, lavishly attired guests–and Jobs, who had left Atari to start Apple in 1976. While everyone was dressed up for party.

Bushnell remembers "sitting on the Left Bank, me sipping coffee and Steve always drinking tea, sort of watching Paris walk by. We had a delightful conversation about the importance of creativity. He was at a phase where he knew that the Apple II was nearing the end of its life. He was not happy with the Apple III. He was just starting to kick around the ideas for the Lisa and what was going to be the Macintosh. **We were talking about trackballs and joysticks and mice, and the whole idea of having a little hand in the screen, which is essentially what the mouse was.**

"I last saw him a year before his death. He was very, very thin, but he didn't look frail. He had a strength about him. He said, 'I think I'm going to beat this thing.'"

Apologetic dealer[150]

In 1998 my wife and I bought five iMacs as Christmas gifts for our grandchildren. We watched them open their presents, and when 5-year-old Molly opened her iMac, she said, **'Life is good.' Unfortunately, Molly's iMac developed a problem. After using it a few hours, the disc drive door would not open.** The dealer told me he was not authorized to exchange the computer for another one due to an Apple policy. Repair would take several weeks, he told me.

I sent an e-mail to Steve and asked him about Apple's return/exchange policy on a new product. Within five minutes my phone rang. It was Steve. He asked me what the problem was and the name of the dealer. 'I'll call you back,' he said. A few minutes later the phone rang and it was a very apologetic dealer. 'I have a new iMac here for your granddaughter,' he said. I e-mailed Steve, thanking him and assuring him that he had made my granddaughter's Christmas a happy one. Steve immediately replied with a simple 'Ho, ho, ho.'

Product secret at all costs[151]

Shortly before Jobs and Apple unveiled the original iPhone at MacWorld in 2007, a group of engineers from the iPhone team went to Jobs' home to debug a problem with the phone's Wi-Fi. At one point while the team was working, a FedEx employee buzzed outside the house to deliver a package to Jobs.

"Steve goes out to meet him because he has to sign for this package, but he's got the iPhone in one of his hands," said a former Apple employee was with the iPhone team at the time. "Steve just walks out casually, [hides] the phone behind his back, signs the package, and the FedEx dude marches off."

The idea that Jobs would walk outside carrying an iPhone in plain sight shocked this employee, given how much effort Apple put into keeping the product secret at all costs.

"You have to understand, when we carried the phones to his house, we carried them in these Pelican lock boxes. These phones were never to leave Apple's campus, and Steve just casually throws it behind his back. That was the first time I saw someone casually come close to seeing the iPhone before it was announced, and he didn't even know it. If the FedEx guy had just tilted his head, he would have seen it.

The Good Earth[152]

In the early 1980s, Steve used to eat lunch at **"The Good Earth"**, the now-defunct Cupertino restaurant where I waitressed when I was sixteen. I remember this nerdy young guy who always ordered the Good Earth tostada, served in a whole-wheat tortilla and topped with sprouts. He smiled shyly at me when he asked for more Good Earth tea and drank gallons of the stuff. Steve always sat alone, devouring books and manuals way beyond my limited teenage understanding along with his food. [...]

I called my mom the moment I heard Steve Jobs had died. She was sitting in front of her iMac, from which she has a view of the Cupertino Valley, The Apple headquarters nestled in the middle like a brilliant white palace. She was crying.

"There was a rainbow one day," she sobbed, "that ended right on top of Apple." My mom snapped a photograph. "I wanted to send it to him!" she added. "I meant to send it to him. And now," she stopped suddenly, struggling for control. "Now, he's dead."

Inebriated[153]

When CNBC reporter Jim Goldman interviewed Jobs after Tuesday's Macworld keynote, he passed on a comment from Robbie Bach, entertainment chief at Microsoft, that the Zune 2 is a "worthy alternative to Apple's iPod".

Jobs reply? "Was he inebriated? Do you even know anyone who owns a Zune?"

Connect the dots[154]

Steve Jobs struggled in school. From his early days in elementary school, where he grew frustrated with formal schooling to college, where he dropped out after just one semester, Jobs did not like school because he didn't believe it had practical application in his life.

But not finishing his education didn't stop him from becoming CEO of one of the world's most innovative technological companies. Jobs used some of what he learned in school to help him create many of his Apple products, but he also used life experience.

Jobs preached that no matter what happens in your life—struggles in school or an unsuccessful career path—every aspect will somehow help you down the road.

"Again, you can't connect the dots looking forward; you can only connect them looking backwards," Jobs said. "So you have to trust that the dots will somehow connect in your future. You have to trust in something—your gut, destiny, life, karma, whatever. This approach has never let me down, and it has made all the difference in my life."

Jobs gave an inspiring commencement address at Stanford in 2005.

Secret Steve Jobs¹⁵⁵

But prior to married life, Jobs had played the field.

In college, Jobs dated singer Joan Baez, according to Elizabeth Holmes, a friend and classmate. In **"The Second Coming of Steve Jobs**," Holmes tells biographer Alan Deutschman that Jobs broke up with his serious girlfriend to "begin an affair with the charismatic singer-activist." Holmes confirmed these details to ABC News.

Deutschman's book also says Jobs went on a blind date with Diane Keaton; went out with Lisa Birnbach, author of "The Preppy Handbook;" and hand delivered computers to celebrities he admired.

He also had a less well-known family life. He has a daughter, Lisa Brennan Jobs, born in 1978 with his high school girlfriend, Chris Ann Brennan.

Fortune magazine reported that Jobs denied paternity of Lisa for years, at one point swearing in a court document that he was infertile and could not have children. According to the report, Chris Ann Brennan collected welfare for a time to support the child, until Jobs later acknowledged Lisa as his daughter.

Jobs' reluctance to accept Lisa is ironic since he was given up for adoption as a child and has refused to speak to his biological father, despite the father's efforts to contact Jobs.

Abdulfattah "John" Jandali, a Syrian man who fathered Jobs, had emailed his son a few times in a tentative effort to make contact. The father never called the son because he feared Jobs would think the dad who had given him up was now after his fortune.

And Jobs never responded to his father's emails.

Ex dishes on sex life[156]

Chrisann Brennan first met Steve Jobs in 1972, while they were both students at Homestead HS in Cupertino, Calif. **Over the next five years, they dated off** and on throughout their teens and early 20s. **The two were living together with their friend Daniel Kottke,** a computer engineer and one of the earliest employees of Apple, in 1977, when the company took off.

The two finally ended their romantic relationship for good in late 1977, after Brennan became pregnant with their daughter, Lisa. Brennan worked as a waitress and collected welfare checks to support herself and their baby daughter.

Jobs publicly denied he was Lisa's father for years, even though he took a paternity test in 1979 proving he was the dad. He was paying $500 a month in child support when he told Time magazine in 1983, "28 percent of the male population in the United States could be the father."

Today, Brennan a painter and graphic designer living in Monterey, Calif., and Lisa is a Harvard-educated journalist.

Steve often said that he had a strong sense of having had a past life as a World War II pilot. He'd tell me how, when driving, he felt a strong impulse to pull the steering wheel back as if for take-off. It was a curious thing for him to say, but he did have that sense of unadorned glamour from the forties. He loved the big band sound of Tommy Dorsey, Benny Goodman, and Count Basie.

At the first Apple party he even danced like he was from the forties. So I could see the fit: Steve as a young man with all that American ingenuity from a less encumbered time, with that simple sense of right and wrong. But that's not how I pictured him in 1977.

Adopted[157]

Jobs was born in San Francisco on February 24, 1955. **He was adopted shortly after his birth and reared near Mountain View, California by a couple named Clara and Paul Jobs.** His adoptive father — a term that Jobs openly objected to — was a machinist for a laser company and his mother worked as an accountant.

Later in life, Jobs discovered the identities of his estranged parents. His birth mother, Joanne Simpson, was a graduate student at the time and later a speech pathologist; his biological father, Abdulfattah John Jandali, was a Syrian Muslim who left the country at age 18 and reportedly now serves as the vice president of a Reno, Nevada casino. While Jobs reconnected with Simpson in later years, he and his biological father remained estranged.

College dropout[158]

The lead mind behind the most successful company on the planet never graduated from college, in fact, he didn't even get close. After graduating from high school in Cupertino, California — a town now synonymous with 1 Infinite Loop, Apple's headquarters — Jobs enrolled in Reed College in 1972. Jobs stayed at Reed (a liberal arts university in Portland, Oregon) for only one semester, **dropping out quickly due to the financial burden the private school's steep tuition placed on his parents.**

In his famous 2005 commencement speech to Stanford University, Jobs said of his time at Reed: "It wasn't all romantic. I didn't have a dorm room, so I slept on the floor in friends' rooms, I returned coke bottles for the 5 cent deposits to buy food with, and I would walk the seven miles across town every Sunday night to get one good meal a week at the Hare Krishna temple."

Job at Atari[159]

Jobs is well known for his innovations in personal computing, mobile tech, and software, but he also helped create one of the best known video games of all-time. In 1975, **Jobs was tapped by Atari to work on the Pong-like game Breakout.**

He was reportedly offered $750 for his development work, with the possibility of an extra $100 for each chip eliminated from the game's final design. Jobs recruited Steve Wozniak (later one of Apple's other founders) to help him with the challenge. Wozniak managed to whittle the prototype's design down so much that Atari paid out a $5,000 bonus — but Jobs kept the bonus for himself, and paid his unsuspecting friend only $375, according to Wozniak's own autobiography.

Wife, Laurene[160]

Like the rest of his family life, Jobs kept his marriage out of the public eye. Thinking back on his legacy conjures images of him commanding the stage in his trademark black turtleneck and jeans, and those solo moments are his most iconic. But at home in Palo Alto, **Jobs was raising a family with his wife, Laurene, an entrepreneur who attended the University of Pennsylvania's prestigious Wharton business school and later received her MBA at Stanford, where she first met her future husband.**

For all of his single-minded dedication to the company he built from the ground up, Jobs actually skipped a meeting to take Laurene on their first date: "I was in the parking lot with the key in the car, and I thought to myself, 'If this is my last night on earth, would I rather spend it at a business meeting or with this woman?' I ran across the parking lot, asked her if she'd have dinner with me. She said yes, we walked into town and we've been together ever since."

In 1991, Jobs and Powell were married in the Ahwahnee Hotel at Yosemite National Park, and the marriage was officiated by Kobin Chino, a Zen Buddhist monk.

Sister[161]

Later in his life, Jobs crossed paths with his biological sister while seeking the identity of his birth parents. **His sister, Mona Simpson (born Mona Jandali), is the well-known author** of anywhere But Here — a story about a mother and daughter that was later adapted into a film starring Natalie Portman and Susan Sarandon.

After reuniting, Jobs and Simpson developed a close relationship. Of his sister, he told a New York Times interviewer: "We're family. She's one of my best friends in the world. I call her and talk to her every couple of days.'' Anywhere But Here is dedicated to "my brother Steve."

Romantic connection[162]

In The Second Coming of Steve Jobs, an unauthorized biography, a friend from Reed reveals that Jobs had a brief fling with folk singer Joan Baez. Baez confirmed the two were close "briefly," though her **romantic connection with Bob Dylan is much better known** (Dylan was the Apple icon's favourite musician). The biography also notes that Jobs went out with actress Diane Keaton briefly.

First Daughter[163]

When he was 23, **Jobs and his high school girlfriend Chris Ann Brennan conceived a daughter,** Lisa Brennan Jobs. **She was born in 1978,** just as Apple began picking up steam in the tech world. He and Brennan never married, and Jobs reportedly denied paternity for some time, going as far as stating that he was sterile in court documents. He went on to father three more children with Laurene Powell. After later mending their relationship, Jobs paid for his first daughter's education at Harvard. She graduated in 2000 and now works as a magazine writer.

Lifestyle[164]

In a few interviews, Jobs hinted at his early experience with the psychedelic drug LSD. Of Microsoft founder Bill Gates, Jobs said: "I wish him the best, I really do. I just think he and Microsoft are a bit narrow. He'd be a broader guy if he had dropped acid once or gone off to an ashram when he was younger."

The connection has enough weight that Albert Hofmann, the Swiss scientist who first synthesized (and took) LSD, appealed to Jobs for funding for research about the drug's therapeutic use.

In a book interview, Jobs called his experience with the drug "one of the two or three most important things I have done in my life." As Jobs himself has suggested, LSD may have contributed to the "think different" approach that still puts Apple's designs a head above the competition.

Jobs will forever be a visionary, and his personal life also reflects the forward-thinking, alternative approach that vaulted Apple to success. During a trip to India, Jobs visited a well-known ashram and returned to the U.S. as a Zen Buddhist.

Jobs was also a pescetarian who didn't consume most animal products, and didn't eat meat other than fish. A strong believer in Eastern medicine, he sought to treat his own cancer through alternative approaches and specialized diets before reluctantly seeking his first surgery for a cancerous tumour in 2004.

Fortune[165]

As the CEO of the world's most valuable brand, Jobs pulled in a comically low annual salary of just $1. While the gesture isn't unheard of in the corporate world — Google's Larry Page, Sergey Brin, and Eric Schmidt all pocketed the same 100 penny salary annually — Jobs has kept his salary at $1 since 1997, the year he became Apple's lead executive. Of his salary, Jobs joked in 2007: "I get 50 cents a year for showing up, and the other 50 cents is based on my performance."

In early 2011, Jobs owned 5.5 million shares of Apple. After his death, Apple shares were valued at $377.64 — a roughly 43-fold growth in valuation over the last 10 years that shows no signs of slowing down.

He may only have taken in a single dollar per year, but Jobs leaves behind a vast fortune. The largest chunk of that wealth is the roughly $7 billion from the sale of Pixar to Disney in 2006. In 2011, with an estimated net worth of $8.3 billion, **he was the 110th richest person in the world, according to Forbes.** If Jobs hadn't sold his shares upon leaving Apple in 1985 (before returning to the company in 1996), he would be the world's fifth richest individual.

While there's no word yet on plans for his estate, Jobs leaves behind three children from his marriage to Laurene Jobs (Reed, Erin, and Eve), as well as his first daughter, Lisa Brennan-Jobs.

Apple Likes[166]

When asked **why he had named his company Apple**, he said: "Because it came before Atari in the phone book." Jobs worked for Atari before starting Apple and he also said that he likes apples and that they had to come up with a name by 5 o'clock that day.

Disagreement for Job Fired[167]

Why was he fired from his own company? Everyone knows that in 1985 Steve Jobs was fired from Apple. Some might even know that it had to do with a fallout between Steve and John Sculley, Apple's CEO at the time, but few know exactly in what consisted the disagreement. Well, **Steve Jobs wanted to drop the price of the then underperforming Macintosh and shift large portion of the advertising budget away from Apple 2 over to the Mac. Sculley disagreed.** He argued that price had no bearing into Macintosh's poor sales, but rather the unimpressive software it ran. Sculley took the matter to the Apple's Board of Directors which sided with the former Pepsi CEO, thus firing Jobs.

Blue boxes[168]

Before starting Apple, **Steve Jobs and Steve Wozniak built and sold digital blue boxes**, a $100 equipment that could hack telephone systems and allowed them make calls to any number in the world. One of their first calls they made using the blue box was to the Vatican with Wozniak pretending to be Henry Kissinger, they asked to talk to the pope. Without success.

Floating point BASIC[169]

Steve Jobs calls one of the mysteries of life how his friend and Apple's Co-founder Steve Wozniak never built a floating point BASIC for the Apple II, despite Jobs having begged him for several weeks to do it. As a result of Wozniak's refusal, **Job reached out to Microsoft to license Bill Gates' BASIC**.

Apple and Adobe[170]

In the early 80s, Steve Jobs visited Adobe Systems. Impressed with their technology, Jobs made an offer to Adobe Co-founder Charles Geschke to buy the company and integrate it into Apple. Geschke refused it. Apple and Adobe had a very good professional relationship until Apple of Steve, by the end of the first decade of 21st century, decide to **rid their very commercially successful mobile devices of Adobe's Flash**.

LSD[171]

He took LSD in his younger days and had no regrets. In a book interview, Jobs called his experience with the drug "one of the two or three most important things I have done in my life." As Jobs himself has suggested, **LSD may have contributed to the "think different" approach** that still puts Apple's designs a head above the competition.

Parents were two graduate[172]

His parents were two graduate students who were perhaps not ready for a child and put him up for adoption. The one requirement his biological parents had was that he be adopted by two college educated people. His adoptive parents were Clara and Paul Jobs.

Another child[173]

His biological parents went on to have another child, Mona Simpson, whom he later met and connected with. **Jobs was a pescetarian** which meant he ate fish but no other meat.

Jobs[174]

Jobs lied to Steve Wozniak. When they made Breakout for Atari, Wozniak and Jobs were going to split the pay 50-50. **Atari gave Jobs $5000 to do the job.** He told Wozniak he got $700 so Wozniak took home $350.

At the tender age of 12, Jobs asked William Hewlett, co-founder of Hewlett-Packard for some parts to complete a school project. Hewlett offered Jobs an internship at his company.

High school[175]

Jobs met Apple co-founder Steve Wozniak in high school when Jobs was 13 and Wozniak was. Steve had a **brief fling with Joan Boaz**, the folk singer back in his hippie days. Unfortunately though, she left him for his favourite musician – Bob Dylan. His Full Name is **Steven Paul Jobs.**

We'll lose our money[176]

"We'll lose our money, but at least we'll have had a company." It's quite easy to fall into the mistake of thinking that the at the creation of Apple, now one of the top two largest companies in the world, the founders were these amazing visionaries filled with conviction of success and their ability to change the world with the product they had created. Well, it certainly wasn't the case with Apple. In fact, both Steve Jobs and Steve Wozniak were pretty certain of how improbable were their chances of success. "We won't see the money we've invested in back," said Wozniak. Jobs replied: "Yeah, we'll lose our money, but at least we will be able to say we had a company."

Blueprints[177]

When he returned to Apple in the mid-90s, Steve Jobs donated Apple's first computers, machines, blueprints to Stanford University. Clearing up the old to make space for the new. That was his way of letting go of the past and embracing the future of then seriously troubled company.

Zero[178]

Following the success of Apple II and subsequent IPO, one of Apple's engineers went to Steve Jobs and told him he would give stock to another employee if Jobs matched it. Jobs replied: "Yeah, I'll match it. **I'll give zero and you give zero.**"

Marriage[179]

His Religion is **Zen Buddhism.** He went to India to meditate and learn about a simpler way of life. He was very private about his marriage. His **wife was Laurene Powell Jobs and they got married in Yosemite national park on March 18, 1991**.

Wife MBA graduate[180]

His wife is an MBA graduate of Stanford and **was appointed by President Obama to be a member of the White House Council for Community Solutions** due to her active involvement in the non-profit community.

Charitable works[181]

Despite his wife's work in the non-profit sector, **Jobs was not known for his charitable works**. In the early days of Apple, Jobs cut back on all of their philanthropic programs saying they would "wait until [they] are profitable." Although they never restarted their programs, they may have donated anonymously.

Excitement[182]

The excitement you feel when opening up a new Apple product is not by accident. **Jobs was passionate about packaging** and a group in the company obsessively open boxes in an attempt to get the right emotional response.

First Apple logo[183]

Apple had three founders, not two. The company was founded in 1976 by Steve Jobs, Steve Wozniak and Ronald Wayne. The **first Apple logo was drawn by Ronald Wayne** who also wrote the original partnership agreement and the Apple I computer manual. Unfortunately, he sold his 10% stake two weeks into the partnership for just $800.

White colour[184]

Jobs did not want to offer products in white. However, after designer Jonathan Ive showed him the shade "moon grey", he was convinced. **Steve Wozniak ended his full-time employment in 1987.** However, he is still an official Apple employee and receives a stipend estimated to be worth $120,000 a year.

Night shift¹⁸⁵

Jobs **purchased Pixar Animation Studios from George Lucas in 1986**.Jobs attended **Reed College** in Portland, Oregon in 1972.While working at Atari, **Jobs was actually put on the night shift because of his hygiene or lack thereof.** It is said that he never bathed, and would walk around the office in his bare feet.

License plates[186]

Jobs **never used license plates on the silver Mercedes SL55 AMG** he always drove. He would **always park in the handicap parking zone**.

School Structure[187]

Steve Jobs **GPA was 2.65 / 4** which is considered pretty mediocre. **Jobs never thought of himself a good student and instead preferred to learn in different ways and didn't enjoy much for the structure of schools.**

Signature inside[188]

Steve Jobs' signature was inside every original Macintosh. Jobs would get the team to sign a piece of paper which would become the model for a metal plate that would go inside every Macintosh computer.

Mentor[189]

Jobs **acted as a mentor to Google founders Sergey Brin and Larry Page** after seeing the potential in the company. Jobs **took on Eric Schmidt, the company's eventual CEO choice, as one of his board members at Apple.**

Business[190]

Jobs felt betrayed by his former apprentices from Google after the company entered the phone market with its Android devices. **He said "Apple didn't enter the search business, so why did Google get into the phone business?"**

First Computer Price[191]

Apple I was the company's first computer and was priced at $666.66.
Steve Wozniak priced it without realizing the devilish connotations, instead
pricing the machine one-third over the wholesale price of $500 and preferring
one repeating digit as it was easier to type. **Older Apple laptops used to
have the logo upside down**. It wasn't a mistake, but a user-friendliness
decision.

Actual apple[192]

The **Apple Macintosh computer was named after an actual apple, the McIntosh**, because this was Jef Raskin's (an Apple employee working on the Macintosh project) favourite variety.

Last words[193]

After ending a long battle with pancreatic cancer, **Jobs' last words were "Oh wow. Oh wow. Oh wow"** while looking over the shoulders of his family. Mona Simpson, revealed this in her eulogy which was published in the New York Times.

Public encounters[194]

Steve Jobs handles public encounters with a mixture of brazenness and celebrity caution, according...

It would seem, based on the emails and comments we've received, **that Jobs is able to mingle freely in public,** albeit with an eye on the exits in case things get awkward or dangerous. Like our colleague Brian Lam over at Gizmodo, we're coming around to the idea that the Jobs-Schmidt coffee might not have been staged. **Jobs and Schmidt are regulars at the café where they were spotted, according to a source Lam quoted last night.**

Publicity Stunt[195]

A lot of writers, including me, suspected the **Steve Jobs and Eric Schmidt meeting in public was a...**

Our readers, meanwhile, tell us Jobs is regularly out and about in Silicon Valley and New York. He's not afraid to cut in line, dine alone, or speed around corners in the Apple parking lot. He does his own dishes. **And sometimes security guards make him show his ID, just like anyone else.**

No fucking Blue[196]

I was working as a bagger at the Palo Alto Whole Foods in the summer of '97 [he probably means '98, when the iMac debuted in August]. I was shagging carts one afternoon when I saw this silver Mercedes parked in a handicapped spot. Steve Jobs was inside screaming at his car phone. This was right before the first iMac was unveiled and I'm pretty sure I could make out, "**Not. Fucking. Blue. Enough**!!!"

Update: The commenter clarifies that while Jobs was yelling, he was joking/speculating about what Jobs actually said. Thus the "Not Fucking Blue Enough" quote above should be discounted.

Parking[197]

A couple years ago, I had a networking-type breakfast with a friend of a friend who worked for Apple, in the main cafeteria on the company's campus in Cupertino. After I'd finished my tasty chorizo omelette (Apple has an amazing omelette bar), **my guy on the inside walked me back to my car.**

We started saying our goodbyes, **and I wasn't really paying attention to where I was standing. Suddenly a silver Mercedes roadster-type car with no license plates came screaming around a bend and swerved ever so slightly to avoid me.**

And my Apple guy said: "Do you know who that was who almost ran you over?"

It was an honour to have impeded your trip to your parking spot, Mr Jobs.

Demo[198]

I was sent to the Apple campus to do a **demo for the Final Cut group in 'the Piano Bar'.** We had a Genelec surround system sent directly to our contact at Apple and I loaded this on a huge cart along with other hardware and my Warr Guitar strapped to my back. We 'booked' the room so we were sure it would be abandoned, including the allocated setup time.

So, I come crashing into this room with the cart *KERBLAM* and I see a group of five people talking quietly at a table in the back. I begin to unload and set up.

Our Apple contact says, "We should, uh, get out of here."

I shrug and follow him out. He and my co-worker leave to go do something and I'm sitting outside the piano bar making sure nobody walks off with my gear. Moments later four, ashen Apple employees scurry out of the room and head out the door followed by a scruffy unshaven fellow. He stops, surveys the area, and, like a missile locking on to a strong heat signature, zeroes in and walks towards me, the person who burst in on the private meeting.

It is funny how the brain works. As this person approached me, I had time to string the following thoughts together: "This guy is coming to talk to me. Heh. His kind of looks like Steve Jobs, but Steve wouldn't wear torn jeans and have a three day beard and what are the chances that within 15 minutes I'd bump into... OMFG..."

He holds out his hand and says, "Hi, I'm Steve."

Fellow patient[199]

I don't personally have a Steve Jobs sighting, but my friend did, probably about four years ago. She lives in downtown Palo Alto a few blocks away from University Avenue, same neighborhood as him. **She was recovering from chemo (she has cancer) and was taking a walk with her husband near the house when they ran into a man who noticed her headscarf and asked her how her treatment was going. They discussed their respective cancer treatments for a while; after he'd moved on, her husband told her who she'd been talking to.**

Also, it's not surprising that he got lost going to the movies. I grew up on the Peninsula, and it happens to me every time I try to go to those big AMC theatres in Mountain View or Cupertino. Imagine a huge parking lot with no obvious landmarks and all the buildings looking indistinguishable from each other. It's not like trying to find the AMC in Union Square!!!

Food line[200]

I never realized that he had a problem being in public. I was getting a smoothie at Whole Foods a few years ago in downtown Palo Alto one day and **guess who was in line in front of me!** After I ordered I went to sit down at the tables and there he was again, eating like a normal person. No bodyguards and no disguises. I mean, he lives in Palo Alto so why would it be weird to see him at a cafe there? First and
last time I've ever seen him (I live in San Jose now).

King

Not sure if this qualifies, but as a former Apple employee, Jobs was knows to park in the first spot closest to the door - even though it was a handicap spot! HR finally had to tell him that isn't OK even for him. Eventually they chalked a spot marked "Jobs" for him.

Also, in the company cafeteria, there could be a HUGE line, however he would rush in and get his food by just cutting in line. It's good to be the king!

Clueless[202]

Not 100% sure if this is what you were looking for, but in 1998, the first year Macworld moved from the two convention centres in Boston to the Javits Centre in New York City, I was walking around the lobby area trying to make my way back onto the convention floor. I was 13 at the time, playing with my 4 year old Newton 120 which my dad had given to me.

Now back in 1998 Steve Job wasn't supposed to show up for the Keynote, he was going to do it via satellite [this is true], but much to my amazement however I see 10 feet in front of me, Steve Jobs.

I'm standing there watching the CEO of Apple and his 4-5 deep entourage yelling at the security guard. As I moved closer I heard one of the entourage say **"This is Steve Jobs, he is the CEO of Apple Computer" to which the guard replied "He is not the CEO of the Javits Centre, he needed a badge to enter." So it seems in his last minute choice to go to Macworld, no one got Mr Jobs and badge. Whoops.**

No hand shake[203]

He met a friend of mine at some huge geek event, and two years later bumped into him at a different event, walked right up, stretched out his hand for a shake and said, "It's Dave, right? From SFU?"

Don't make Steve Jobs shake your hand, he is sick, you insensitive clod:

Good with Kids²⁰⁴

Many years ago, my family were hanging out at a park near downtown Palo Alto. My kids were running around like they were insane and soon we were joined by several others.

As I am want to do, I turned into a monster and chased the kids bellowing at the top of my lungs and generally acting like the world's largest 7 year old.

One little girl went up to her dad and said 'This is the best park ever! He's so funny!'

Her dad was Steve Jobs.

He was warm, friendly and thanked me for running his kids ragged at the park. His wife was nice too.

My brush with awesomeness.

He's good with kids, when his mind doesn't wander:

My first Steve Jobs sighting took place at Stanford Shopping Centre, in Palo Alto, California, in the fall of 2002.

It was on a Saturday, in the heart of the Christmas shopping season. I was sitting with two of my teenaged cousins at one of the outdoor cafes, La Baguette, when Steve walked by with one of his children. I noticed him right away because he was wearing his black turtleneck and blue jeans, as well as his wire-rimmed eyeglasses [...]

Another thing I observed: As he strode along with his child, he seemed much focused — as if on a mission to get someplace by a certain time. And though he was holding his child's hand — which I thought was cute, on his part — he also appeared not to notice his child was walking next to him.

PS — Since then, I've seen him a number of times during visits to Apple HQ — particularly inside IL 1 and at Cafe Mac — usually alone, though once with Jonny Ive.

Vehicle care[205]

Hello, I live in Mountain View, CA right next door to his home town of Palo Alto, and occasionally drive by his house on Waverly. One time my wife and I drove by and saw him outside either washing or waxing his SL 55—can't remember, this was a few years ago, I think even before the iPhone. **He looked in our direction as we drove by, and nodded as he probably noticed that both of us were staring, but that was about it.**

Cool on the catwalk.

When the Apple store in SoHo NYC opened, Steve was hanging out chatting with anyone who recognized him (surprisingly few people in NYC cared about him back then). I caught him hanging out on the little bridge connecting the two sides of the upper floor
. **He was just soaking up the launch of his newest baby, taking a moment to enjoy what was undoubtedly a whole lot of hard work. For such a private and allegedly aloof person, he is cool as can be.**

Storyteller[206]

The visionary Apple co-founder was also a **master storyteller** who used narratives to motivate his team.

Steve Jobs knew the power of storytelling better than almost any entrepreneur. In the new book Illuminate: **Ignite Change Through Speeches, Stories, Ceremonies, and Symbols, co-authors Nancy Duarte, CEO of Silicon Valley design firm Duarte, and communications expert Patti Sanchez share how leaders like Jobs have used creative communication methods to bring about change. Here are four innovative ways Jobs inspired Apple's employees with compelling stories, as cited in the book.**

Ceremony[207]

Jobs was known for using symbolic gestures at Apple, like having the signatures of every member of the original Macintosh team engraved on the inside of every Mac (the way artists sign their work), **but he also used ceremonies to help forward his agenda.** For example, when he wanted the company to forget about Mac OS 9 and move on to Mac OS X, he held a mock funeral for Mac OS 9 and even delivered a eulogy.

"Mac OS 9 was a friend to all of us. He worked tirelessly on our behalf, always hosting our applications, **never refusing a command, always at our beck and call, except occasionally when he forgot who he was and needed to be restarted,"** Jobs said. "Mac OS 9 is survived by his next generation, Mac OS X, and thousands of applications, most of them legitimate." This light-hearted ceremony made it clear to all of Apple's developers that the days of developing for the Mac OS 9 were gone.

Not all answer[208]

After creating the original Mac OS, which fell short of giving consumers everything they wanted in a modern operating system, Jobs told a story about seeing a Xerox presentation in 1979. The first of three features unveiled at the presentation, Xerox's graphical interface, was truly revolutionary, but it was followed by two other OS features that Jobs didn't fully appreciate at the time. "I was so blinded by the first that I didn't hang around to find out about the other two, and it took me years to rediscover them," Jobs said.

Similarly, at an Apple presentation where Jobs had to apologize to developers for terminating several products they had spent months working on, an angry developer stood up and told Jobs he didn't know what he was talking about. **Instead of arguing with the developer, Jobs said: "People like this gentleman are right in some areas." The lesson? Acknowledging your critics doesn't necessarily undermine your ability to lead.**

Audience[209]

People want to be a part of something exciting--but they also want to know that others are willing to be a part of it, too. To encourage a group of wary developers to build applications for a new Macintosh platform, **Jobs told a story about a software developer who had already made the switch.** "This is a developer I've known for a long time. I gave him a call and I said, 'We've got something really secret we're working on and I can't tell you what it is, but I want you to put all your source code on a hard disc and fly out here... I think you're going to be very pleasantly surprised." By telling a story of a developer taking a leap of faith and being pleased with the result, Jobs demonstrated that other developers could have the same experience.

Listen more[210]

At the World Wide Developers Conference in 1997, Jobs knew some developers would be angry about the acquisition of NeXT, and the changes that would come with using the NeXT OS. Instead of giving his usual presentation, Jobs turned the mic on the audience to hear their stories. **"I want to talk about whatever you want to talk about,"** he said. **By listening and expressing empathy in a town hall format--instead of citing all the reasons going with the NeXT OS was the right move--Jobs cut the tension in the room and gave his developers the opportunity to vent their frustrations.**

Whether or not you agree with the criticism over Jobs' management style, which has been described as manipulative and maniacal, the fact remains: **The man knew how to grab people--consumers, partners, and employees--with a great story. And that's something every entrepreneur should learn.**

Responsible parent[211]

Apple may make the world's most in-demand Christmas presents, but Steve Jobs was not a complete technology evangelist -- **he strictly limited the amount of time his children got to use tech.** Asked in 2010 if his own children loved the iPad, he said: "They haven't used it. We limit how much technology our kids use at home." **Children in the Jobs house were required to sit down at dinner and talk with the family.**

Office remains[212]

Speaking to Charlie Rose this last weekend, Apple CEO, Tim Cook said: "I literally think about him every day. **His office is still left as it was,**" Cook says. **"His name is still on the door."**

"He stood for innovation. He stood for the simple not the complex. He knew Apple should only enter areas in which it could control the primary technology."

Commencement speech inside Mac[213]

Apple has hidden the full text of Steve Jobs' famous Stanford University commencement speech inside every Mac. **Just press Command + Shift + G while in Finder to open the Go to Folder box, and paste the following:/Applications/Pages.app/Contents/Resources/**

Open the file called Apple.txt and read the speech.

Great Teacher[214]

Cook also told Charlie Rose he doesn't think anything written so far about Steve Jobs fully captures him. **"He was one of the best mentors in the world," said Cook. "He was a great teacher. This is something that's never written about him,"** he added, explaining Jobs would work hard to try to ensure people understood what he was trying to teach them.

Amazed by Xerox[215]

A little-known video clip offers an eye-witness account of what happened when Steve Jobs visited Xerox PARC in winter 1979 where he was first shown the graphical user interface and computer mouse. The speaker is ex-PARC scientist, Larry Tesler who says: **"Steve got very excited. He was pacing around the room, occasionally looking at the screen... He was mostly taking it all in, trying to process it."**

Jobs also said: "What is going on here? You're sitting on a gold mine! Why aren't you doing something with this technology? You could change the world!"

The clip makes it crystal clear Apple did not "steal" the Xerox technology, instead a mutually profitable deal was reached.

Convinced Apple[216]

Jobs wasn't going to become CEO of Apple after he re-joined the company in '96. Instead he spoke with potential hires, including Joe Costello, now CEO of Enlightened and formerly the boss of Cadence Design Systems. **Costello says that after a few hours discussing the Apple CEO position Jobs wanted him to fill, he realized Jobs had more passion for the company than anyone else.** So he asked him: "Look Steve, the best way to find a person for any job is to think of the absolute best guy on the planet for that job. Who do you think is the best person in the world?"

Jobs went silent and looked to Costello and said, "I am".

Costello pointed out that Jobs should not be recruiting for a CEO when he wanted to be CEO himself. Apple eventually gave Jobs the job and the rest is history.

Apple Watch[217]

Work on Apple Watch development began after Jobs died, said Cook in an interview last week: "You know we started working on it after his passing, but his DNA runs through all of us," Cook said.

I hope you have enjoyed this short collection. I believe it is possible to build a better picture of the man than we have so far.

Second comeback[218]

What is generally considered the best, and last, intimate profile of Jobs published in a magazine was written by Joe Nocera for Esquire's December 1986 issue—**(Jobs had been fired by Apple a little more than a year earlier and was starting his new computer company, NeXT.)**

One moment he's kneeling in his chair, the next minute he's slouching in it; the next he has leaped out of his chair entirely and is scribbling on the blackboard directly behind him. He is full of mannerisms. **He bites his nails.** He stares with unnerving earnestness at whoever is speaking. **His hands, which are slightly and inexplicably yellow, are in constant motion: pushing back his hair, propping up his chin, buried snugly under his armpits. When he hears something that intrigues him, he curls his head toward his shoulder, leans forward, and allows a slight smile to cross his lips.** When he hears something he dislikes, he squints to register his disapproval. He would not be a good poker player. His speech is also mannered, full of slangy phrases. "If we could pull this off," he is saying enthusiastically, "it would be really, really neat!" **"The original idea was good,"** he is saying about some failed project at Apple. "I don't know what happened. I guess somebody there bozoed out." Around the room there are knowing smirks. **To bozo is a favourite Jobs verb,** but where he once used it mainly to describe some bit of stupidity perpetrated by, say, IBM, he now uses it just as often when he's talking about Apple.

In 2008, Esquire profiled Jobs again, without his cooperation, on the occasion of his first public appearance in several months—at Apple's annual Worldwide Developers Conference—amid rumours about his health.

Portal[219]

And that's why the spectacle of Steve Jobs introducing the iPhone 3G in June was so moving. It wasn't just that he was withered, and that his black mock turtleneck was bunching up like a flag on a listless day; it was that Steve Jobs was withering within the idea of himself. Gaunt as a pirate, dressed in what had heretofore been the vestments of his invulnerability, he was still speaking in the voice of a boy- inventor from a Mickey Rooney movie, he was still talking about Apple's **"really great ... really beautiful ..."** products, he was still the Alpha Adolescent, he was still making his bid in the only way he knew how. And the bid—for immortality, for influence, for a multiplication of himself both within and without the terms of himself—was, in the form of the improved iPhone, there in the palm of his hand, which is precisely where he's always wanted it... . Except it was clear that, in this case, he had started something he might not be able to finish. **Not just because he was so sick, but rather because the iPhone was so alive.**

Invitation to Fan boy [220]

Growing up I was a huge apple fan-boy (fine, still am.) The first NY apple store in Soho opening was probably the coolest thing that happened to me between the ages 6 and 12. For a while I would spend almost every weekend there. Every year for Halloween I was a mac, and I made a habit of shaving the Apple logo into my head to celebrate every OS launch.

My neighbour Brooke mentioned that Steve Jobs, busy as he is, always reads email sent to his public address. **I think I was around 10 or 12, and I sent a very enthusiastic and grammatically incorrect message including a picture of my shaved head [with an Apple logo in the back).**

Apparently he forwarded it to the head of Public Relations, Katie [Cotton], and I got invited to the opening of the 5th Avenue Cube. I can never thank them enough. This was probably the high point of my childhood.

ALS²²¹

In 1998, Jobs decided that Airborne Logistics Services, a division of Airborne Express that maintained a parts warehouse for Apple in Grove City, Ohio, wasn't delivering spare parts quickly enough. According to Jeff Cooke, who ran Apple's customer-service department at the time, Jobs ordered him to find a **replacement for ALS.** When Cooke resisted, citing concerns that ALS would sue for breach of contract, he says Jobs told him that "there won't be any lawsuit. Just tell them if they f--- with us, they'll never get another f---ing dime from this company, ever," Cooke recalls. Jobs says he does not remember making the comment, but confirms that he was determined to drop ALS.

Sure enough, Apple became embroiled in a **lawsuit with ALS,** which was settled in mid-1999. Cooke resigned after just 100 days at Apple. "My stock options would be worth $10 million had I stayed, but I knew I couldn't have stood it--and he'd have fired me anyway," says Cooke. If some of Jobs methods are distasteful, they do get results. After dumping ALS, Apple gave its spare-parts business to PC Service Source and demanded it slash the inventory by 75% in a matter of weeks, says former PC Service Source CEO Mark Hilz, now head of a Dallas real estate management company. **"They got very, very, very results-oriented once Jobs got back there," says Hilz. "Under Steve Jobs, there's zero tolerance for not performing."**

Microsoft problem[222]

"The only problem with Microsoft is they just have no taste," he said last year in "Triumph of the Nerds," a television documentary about the history of the computer industry. "I don't mean that in a small way. I mean that in a big way, in the sense that they don't think of original ideas and they don't bring much culture into their products. I have no problem with their success -- they've earned their success for the most part. I have a problem with the fact that they just make really third-rate products."

The statement was quintessential Jobs: arrogant, frank, insightful and perhaps more than half right, though brutally overstated. Those same traits were both his strength and his weakness at Apple. After the documentary was televised, Jobs called Gates to apologize, sort of. "I told him I believed every word of what I'd said but that I never should have said it in public," Jobs says. "I wish him the best, I really do. I just think he and Microsoft are a bit narrow. He'd be a broader guy if he had dropped acid once or gone off to an ashram when he was younger."

Passion for work223

I should tell you this story. We're in a meeting at NeXT, before Steve went back to Apple. I've got my chief scientist. **After the meeting, we leave and try to unravel the argument to figure out where Steve was wrong—because he was obviously wrong. And we couldn't do it. We're standing in the parking lot.**

He sees us from his office, and he comes back out to argue with us some more. It was over a technical issue involving Objective C, a computer language. Why he would care about this was beyond me. I've never seen that kind of passion.

Employee number[224]

Business Insider: What is the significance of the employee numbers, since you were saying that you took seven because you wanted it?

Michael Scott (Apple's first CEO): We had to have a payroll, and in order to minimize how much work we had to do, I had to sign up with Bank of America's payroll system, and those days you didn't have a choice. **You had to assign employee numbers.**

That was a dispute you get into — **who gets number 1?** One of the first things was that of course, **each Steve wanted number 1.** I know I didn't give it to Jobs because I thought that would be too much. **I don't remember if it was Woz or Markkula that got number 1, but it didn't go to Jobs because I had enough problems anyway.**

Challenge[225]

I would say that the challenge was, who was more stubborn, Steve or I, and I think I won.

The other argument at the meetings was would **Steve take his dirty feet and sandals off the table,** because he sat at one end of the conference table, and **Markkula sat at the other end chain smoking.** So we had to have special filters in the attic in the ceiling to keep the room filter. I had the smokers on one side and the people with dirty feet on the other.

[Laughter from interviewer.]

It was not funny then. Everybody has their pet peeves.

Penny off[226]

A little side story that he and I would fight over. If we were negotiating price for parts, we could negotiate a price with a vendor and at the last minute, Steve would come in and bang on the table and demand to get **one more penny off. And of course they would give him one more penny off.** Then he'd crow "well I see you didn't do as good a job as you could've getting the price down."

And I'm saying**, "Yeah but that one more penny might've cost us a bit more ill will for times when parts are in short supply."**

Keys[227]

True to form, the shepherd [Steve Jobs] to his Apple flock often teaches in parables. One such lesson could be called the "Difference between the Janitor and the Vice President," and it's a sermon Jobs delivers every time an executive reaches the VP level.

Jobs imagines his garbage regularly not being emptied in his office, and when he asks the janitor why, he gets an excuse: **The locks have been changed, and the janitor doesn't have a key.** This is an acceptable excuse coming from someone who empties trash bins for a living. The janitor gets to explain why something went wrong. Senior people do not. "When you're the janitor," **Jobs has repeatedly told incoming VPs, "reasons matter."** He continues: "Somewhere between the janitor and the CEO, reasons stop mattering." That "Rubicon," he has said, "is crossed when you become a VP."

History of Silicon Valley[228]

I first met Steve Jobs 13 years ago, when I was working on **book on the history of Silicon Valley.** Following an extended tap dance with his Apple gatekeeper, and **after I'd already interviewed most of the Valley's other leaders, Jobs agreed to see me, in conference room at Apple headquarters. I got to see first-hand what I'd so often heard about: smarts, breadth, charm and abrasiveness.**

Before sitting down, he said, **"You've got 20 minutes,"** adding with some derision, **"You're not from here, are you?"** I asked why he asked, also wondering to myself where he'd honed his social graces. "Look at how you're dressed!" he said. Jobs had on his usual black mock turtleneck and faded jeans. **I was wearing a blue blazer and Oxford shirt. "I was just trying to show you some respect,"** I offered. **He nodded, smiled slightly and acknowledged my efforts.**

We wound up talking for three hours. **I liked him right away,** idiosyncrasies and all. [...] In that initial, back in 1998, Jobs began by going to a whiteboard to draw a biographical timeline of the Valley. There were Bill Hewlett and Dave Packard back in 1938, developing an audio oscillator in their Palo Alto garage, and in the process giving birth to Silicon Valley; there was brilliant-but-pathological William Shockley, who founded the first semiconductor company in 1956, in Mountain View; there were the "Traitorous Eight" -- including Gordon Moore, Bob Noyce and Gene Kleiner -- who bolted from Shockley to launch Fairchild Semiconductor in 1957, which led to the most famous of the "Fair children" spin-offs, a company called Intel, started by Moore and Noyce in 1968, as well as the Valley's first major venture-capital firm, Kleiner Perkins Caufield & Byers, co-founded by Kleiner and Tom Perkins four years later.

Second meeting[229]

The second time I met Steve Jobs was on a Manhattan street corner. He was coming to speak to a group of us at Newsweek and we entered the building at the same time. **It was in 1999, the week after my book on the Valley had come out. "I'm hearing great things about your book, David," he told me.**

"Really?" I said. "That's good to hear. What did you think of the book?"

"Haven't read it -- probably won't." He seemed to say it as a punch line, with some glee.

Joys of parenthood[230]

The last time I saw Jobs was by chance in the courtyard at Apple headquarters 3½ years ago. I was there with my older son, then 15, to have lunch with an Apple friend. My son is a big Apple fan and user. **By chance, we saw Jobs was walking along by himself, pecking away at his iPhone. I said hello, as did he -- and he then took my son aside to chat for several minutes, about technology and thinking large. My son was rapt.**

It was a gracious thing for Jobs to do, with no payoff for himself. (I don't merit efforts to co-opt.) He later e-mailed me about the joys of parenthood. While Jobs was tone-deaf at times, he wasn't a jerk.

Tough[231]

He once [called] your editor, Andy Serwer, at Fortune, and John Huey, when he was trying to kill a story that you may have worked on at Fortune about his cancer treatment and everything else.

And he finally said, "What do you have in the story?" And Serwer told him what's in the book. And he finally said, **"Well, wait a minute, you've discovered that I'm an asshole?** Why is that news?" So, **he was self-aware, he was tough.**

Business Card[232]

He's paid $100,000 to have the logo for NeXT Computer. Paul Rand, who did it, who was a great designer — **[Steve Jobs] said, "I want you to design a business card for me."** It was "Steven P. Jobs." And they fought over whether the period after the P should be under the P, which is what you could do with bitmap displays, or if it should be right afterward, which was the normal way of doing it.

And they fought so badly that Paul Rand would not surrender, and Steve Jobs had it done his own way. This is the passion for detail and perfection that is usually considered a micromanaging passion, but he does connect it, too, to the broad vision. And the broad vision is... **I mean, look, the whole desktop publishing industry comes out of the fact that he cared about fonts.**

Colour

About right when the iPad was about to come out, I fly into San Francisco. And you get off the plane, and the thing you least want to see on your iPhone, which is seven missed phone calls from Steve Jobs.

[...] It wasn't like he was returning my calls. It's like he was mad about something... And Simon & Schuster had put a cover sort of in the catalogue they were putting out two years ago. It had Steve in a red apple, "iSteve," and some day as to when it would be published. He said, **"That is the ugliest thing — this has such poor taste,"** and it was actually words of one syllable that were stronger than that. "You shouldn't even come to the product launch, I never want to deal with you again. **You have no taste,"** and whatever.

Finally, he says, "I'm only going to keep dealing with you if you let me have some input into the cover." **"Because,"** he said, **"nobody is going to read your book, I'm not going to read your book. But I'll look at the cover — and I don't want it to be ugly." Now, it takes me about one and a half seconds to say, "Sure!" I mean, here's a guy with the greatest design eye of our time.**

That is basically Steve Jobs saying, "That's what the cover should look like." With a font that comes from the original Mac, the sans serif font, and the Albert Watson picture, and it's in black and white. And I said, "Shouldn't we do it in colour?" He says, "No, I'm a black and white sort of guy: Things are either black, or they're white. It's a black and white cover."

Great inventions[234]

One time, Steve and I sat in Dr. [Edwin] Land's conference room at his office on the Charles River that he used after he was fired from Polaroid. **I sat there listening while these two geniuses discussed where great inventions come from.**

Pointing toward the centre of the empty conference table, Dr. Land said**, "I didn't invent the Polaroid camera, it's always existed, just waiting to be discovered." Steve replied, "That's right. I knew long before we built it exactly what the Mac was. It always existed.** I never had to ask customers what they wanted. If it's something truly revolutionary, they won't be able to help you." **All of Steve's visionary products have always existed, they were just waiting for him to discover them.**

Keynote[235]

Years ago, I heard the back-story on Apple's switch to Intel first-hand from some folks on the IBM side of things, and what I learned was **that Steve Jobs agonized over this decision and waited until the morning of the keynote before pulling the trigger on this move.**

He actually went into that day with **two keynote presentations prepared: one for a PowerPC-based product line, and one for The Switch.**

When he pulled out The Switch presentation, the IBM team was absolutely as stunned as the rest of the world, as was the P.A. Semi team who had been separately assured by Jobs that their dual-core PowerPC part would find its way into Apple portables.

Pup consultant[236]

He was running NeXT Computer. **I was a young pup consultant who had to tell him his baby was ugly.** My elder colleagues made sure I spoke first so he wouldn't be offended.

After he heard my story, he stood up and did his pitch for the NeXT OS. Just like he always did when he introduced the Macintosh, iMac, iPod, iPhone or iPad – he electrified the crowd with his vision and enthusiasm. For a moment, I thought every fact I collected and put together over the previous two months were from never-never land.

Steve then walked over and thanked me for doing a good job and he said he understood it was time to move on.

Napkin[237]

Anyway, when the was over, he invited me to have dinner with him at a soba-noodle shop in downtown Manhattan. My wife was invited, too, along with his executive-design team. And I kick myself over what happened next. They all —I don't want to say they live in fear of him— are certainly are subservient to his will and whim. But I had no dog in the race I felt much freer to crack jokes and engage him in conversation, which surprised them a bit. At a certain point in the meal, out of nowhere, he turned to his designers and said, "You know what I want to make?" And they all snapped their heads around and replied, **"What, Steve? What, Steve?"**

"You know those picture frames that has my kid in his baseball cap and uniform?"
"Yeah, Steve! Yeah, Steve! We know picture frames!"
"Well, I want to make a picture frame where the picture's not a picture, but a little movie of the kid swinging the bat and hitting the ball. Can we do that?"
"We can do that, Steve!" said the designers in unison.
"I'll show you what I mean."

And he took his napkin and started sketching out the schematics and he passed the napkin around the table. They all approved the design – nobody touched it, there were no changes or suggestions. The check soon came and we started to get up the leave—and the napkin just sat there on the table. I thought to myself, **"I got to take that napkin"** and my hand was on it, but Steve called from the door and asked, **"Noah, you want to share a cab with me?"** So I put the napkin down. I could have had an Edison original.

Gift[238]

I met Jobs at a celebrity-filled birthday party for a youngster in New York City. As the evening progressed, I wandered around to discover that **Jobs had gone off with the nine-year-old birthday boy to give him the gift he'd brought from California: a Macintosh computer.** As I watched, he showed the boy how to sketch with the machine's graphics program. Two other party guests wandered into the room and looked over Jobs shoulder. **'Hmmm,' said the first,** Andy Warhol. **'What is this?** Look at this, Keith. **This is incredible!'** The second guest, Keith Haring, the graffiti artist whose work now commands huge prices, went over. Warhol and Haring asked to take a turn at the Mac, and as I walked away, Warhol had just sat down to manipulate the mouse. **'My God!' he was saying, 'I drew a circle!'**

But more revealing was the scene after the party. Well after the other guests had gone, Jobs stayed to tutor the boy on the fine points of using the Mac. Later, I asked him why he had seemed happier with the boy than with the two famous artists. His answer seemed unrehearsed to me: "Older people sit down and ask, 'What is it?' but the boy asks, 'What can I do with it?'"

World Wide Web[239]

After having written www, [inventor of the World Wide Web] Berners-Lee noticed that **there was a NeXT developers conference in Paris at which Steve Jobs would be present.** Tim packed up his black cube, complete with the optical disk which contained arguably the most influential and important code ever written and took a train to Paris.

It was a large and popular conference and Tim was pretty much at the end of the line of black NeXT boxes. **Each developer showed Steve Jobs their new word-processor, graphic programme and utility and he slowly walked along the line, like the judge at a flower show nodding his approval or frowning his distaste.** Just before he reached Tim and the World Wide Web at the end of the row, an aide nudged Jobs and told him that they should go or he'd be in danger of missing his flight back to America. So Steve turned away and never saw the programme that Tim Berners-Lee had written which would change the world as completely as Gutenberg had in 1450. It was a meeting of the two most influential men of their time that never took place. Chatting to the newly knighted Sir Tim a few years ago he told me that he had still never actually met Steve Jobs.

Cupertino campus meeting[240]

Early on a July workday in 1997, Jim McCluney, then head of Apple's worldwide operations got the call. McCluney was summoned with other top brass of the beleaguered company to **Apple Computer's boardroom on its Cupertino campus.** Embattled Chief Executive Gil Amelio wasted no time. With an air of barely concealed relief, he said: "Well, I'm sad to report that it's time for me to move on. Take care," McCluney recalls. And he left.

A few minutes later, in walked Steve Jobs. The co-founder of the once proud company had been fired by Apple 12 years before. He had returned seven months earlier as a consultant, when Amelio acquired his NeXT Software. And now Jobs was back in charge. Wearing shorts, sneakers, and a few days' growth of beard, he sat down in a swivel chair and spun slowly, says McCluney, now president of storage provider Emulex.

"O.K., tell me what's wrong with this place," Jobs said. After some mumbled replies, he jumped in: **"It's the products! So what's wrong with the products?"** Again, executives began offering some answers. Jobs cut them off. **"The products suck!"** he roared. **"There's no sex in them anymore!"**

Electric conversation[241]

Anyone who doubts the tenacity of Steven P. Jobs gets an earful from his head cheerleader and principal investor, billionaire H. Ross Perot.

Perot tells of a San Francisco party last year where he ran into the King of Spain. When the King asked whom else he should meet there, Perot suggested Jobs. Soon, the King engaged the entrepreneur in what Perot recalls as an **"electric conversation," with Jobs gesturing madly in front of the transfixed monarch. Then the King took out his card, scribbled on the back, and handed it to Jobs. Perot hurried across the room. "What happened?" Replied a beaming Jobs: "I sold him a computer."**

Cube[242]

Job's nagging perfectionism extended to every detail. He insisted on a finish inside the [NeXT] **cube's magnesium shell** -- even though it would never be seen.

He disliked a tiny line left in the chassis by the **moulds for the cube**, a flaw most computer makers deem unavoidable. Jobs flew to Chicago to persuade the die caster to retool. "Not a lot of die casters expect a celebrity to fly in," says Kelley.

Third-party[243]

Guy Kawasaki, another early employee who was assigned to recruit outside developers to write software for the new machine, said Jobs once came by his cubicle with an executive Kawasaki didn't recognize. **Jobs asked for Kawasaki's opinion about some third-party company's software. Kawasaki replied that he didn't think it was very good.** "And Steve turns to the guy and he says, 'See, that's what we think about your product,'" Kawasaki says, laughing. **The stranger was the third-party company's chief executive officer. "I'm sure the CEO did not expect to get ripped like that."**

Photo shoot[244]

Jobs had to have a calla lily. It was 11 p.m. in New York City in December 1983, and he absolutely had to have a calla lily in his suite at the Carlyle Hotel. No other flower would do. He also needed a piano. "Not that he played one," says Andrea Cunningham, who did marketing for Apple. He merely stipulated that his room have one. Cunningham was part of Jobs entourage in town for a **Fortune magazine photo shoot to promote the Mac, which was going to be introduced just a month later on Jan. 24, 1984.**

"He was being such a pill," says Cunningham. "He staunchly refused to do anything the photographer asked." **To lighten the mood, she set up a tape recorder and played music Jobs liked**—the Michael Jackson album Thriller. **No dice; Jobs refused to pose. Then the song Billie Jean came on. "He snapped to and was a different guy,"** she says. **"And as soon as the song ended, he reverted back. So I kept rewinding the tape to play over and over so he'd behave."**

Keynote speech[245]

If Jobs knew NeXT was a loser, he rarely let on. He remained demanding, confident, and grandiose.

Asked to deliver the keynote speech at a computer trade show at the Javits Convention Centre in Manhattan, Jobs told MacAskill to ship out Jobs own desk —complete with the vase and red rose he always kept there—for him to sit at onstage. He insisted that the desk be placed at a 28-degree angle, to match the angle of Rand's box-shaped logo, which was tipped to one side.

A few minutes before the curtains opened, MacAskill begged Jobs not to introduce a new Lotus spreadsheet that hadn't been cleared by Lotus. "Fine," Jobs said, "then you do the speech," and walked off "only to return as the curtain opened." MacAskill says he and everyone else put up with the volatility and withering personal insults because "we really thought we had the chance to change the world."

Room Floppy drive[246]

A few months after taking over, Jobs called operations Chief James M. McCluney and hardware engineering Chief Rubinstein into his office and dramatically lifted a Styrofoam model of what would be the iMac out of a bowling bag. **The duo reported back a few weeks later that it wouldn't work, because they couldn't find room for a floppy drive.** Hardly missing a beat, Jobs said, "No worries. Disk drives are over the hill. CDs are going to get so cheap that no one will miss [floppies]." Says McCluney: "It was remarkable. It was a snap judgment."

Keyboard keys[247]

When I invited Jobs to take some time away from NeXT to speak to a group of students, he sat in the lotus position in front of my fireplace and wowed us for three hours, as if leading a séance.

But then I asked him if he would sign my Apple Extended Keyboard. He burst out: "This keyboard represents everything about Apple that I hate. **It's a battleship. Why does it have all these keys?** Do you use this F1 key? No." And with his car keys he pried it right off. "How about this F2 key?" Off them all went. "I'm changing the world, one keyboard at a time," he concluded in a calmer voice.

Official corporate blue and green colours[248]

On my first day at NeXT, as we walked around the building, my colleagues shared in hushed voices that Jobs personally chose the wood flooring and various appointments. He even specified the outdoor sprinkler system layout.

I witnessed his attention to detail during a marketing reorganization meeting. The VP of marketing read Jobs e-mailed reaction to the new org chart. Jobs simply requested that the charts be reprinted with the **official corporate blue and green colours.** Shifted colour space was like a horribly distorted concerto to his senses.

Call anytime[249]

I never knew when Steve was going to call. But I knew that when he did, it would probably be in the middle of the night.

In 2001 my company was developing Ethernet chips for Mac computers. Steve was enormously excited about our product. He was enormously excited about everything. And restless and sometimes agitated—and frankly, he could be a bit of a pain. **He was like a bulldog.** He worked all the time, day and night, and he expected everyone around him to be that way, too. He insisted that the person at the top or someone who had absolute control was the guy he interfaced with. He demanded that he get as much time as necessary.

If it was 3 in the morning and Steve had a thought or a question or complaint, he picked up the phone and called, right then. The concept of "**that can wait until the morning**" did not apply. **He wasn't going to sleep until he addressed the issue.**

Stage for 9 seconds250

I worked at one point for 72 sleepless hours for something that **Steve Jobs showed on stage for 9 seconds. It's top three, if not No. 1, of my professional achievements.** It didn't look any different on that screen as it did on mine, but it was the knowledge that it was good enough to be on the stage that made it suddenly look different. I'll never get that chance again, and I'm glad I had it.

Online[251]

Steve Jobs was a genius, but he knew his limits. "He was never a guy who tried to make believe he had expertise in something," said Barry Schuler, now a partner at venture capital firm Draper Fisher Jurvetson. That was clear to Schuler when he got a call from Jobs in early 1997 to come over to his old offices at NeXT Software in Redwood City, Calif. Jobs, at that point, hadn't yet agreed to run Apple on a permanent basis.

"What's this Internet thing?" Schuler recalled Jobs asking. "I don't get it. What are people doing on it? **What do they like about it?**"

Schuler, who was AOL's president of creative development at the time, remembered Jobs asking if the excitement was about reading **magazines online.**

"I don't get why anyone would want to read a magazine on a computer screen," he said. **"That's a terrible experience."**

Limestone[252]

Working with Jobs was far from tension-free. **When the limestone that arrived in Cupertino didn't match the sample Jobs had approved, he called to yell at [architect Ronnette Riley] for not checking the shipment personally while in Italy.**

Another time, she was whispering to someone in the corner of the conference room while Jobs was interrogating someone on the other side of the room.

"Suddenly, he turned around and said, 'Could you please be quiet—I'm trying to yell at someone over here!' "Riley said.

Intel Inside' program[253]

Journalist **"Can you say why are you not participating in the 'Intel Inside' program,** putting the stickers on your new or previous Macs?"

Steve Jobs "Huh — but we could... What can I say? We like our own stickers better."

Make iPod Smaller[254]

When engineers were working on the very **first iPod completed the prototype,** they presented their work to Steve Jobs for his approval. **Jobs played with the device, scrutinized it, weighed it in his hands, and promptly rejected it. It was too big.**

The engineers explained that they had to reinvent inventing to create the iPod and **that it was simply impossible to make it any smaller. Jobs was quiet for a moment. Finally he stood, walked over to an aquarium, and dropped the iPod in the tank. After it touched bottom, bubbles floated to the top.**

"Those are air bubbles," he snapped. "That means there's space in there. Make it smaller."

Failed Product[255]

MobileMe was a dud. Users complained about lost e-mails, and syncing was spotty at best. Though reviewers gushed over the new iPhone, they panned the MobileMe service. Steve Jobs doesn't tolerate duds. Shortly after the launch event, he summoned the MobileMe team, gathering them in the Town Hall auditorium in Building 4 of Apple's campus, the venue the company uses for intimate product unveilings for journalists. According to a participant in the meeting, Jobs walked in, clad in his trademark black mock turtleneck and blue jeans, clasped his hands together, and asked a simple question: "Can anyone tell me what MobileMe is supposed to do?" Having received a satisfactory answer, he continued, **"So why the fuck doesn't it do that?"**

For the next half-hour Jobs berated the group. "You've tarnished Apple's reputation," he told them. "You should hate each other for having let each other down." The public humiliation particularly infuriated Jobs. Walt Mossberg, the influential Wall Street Journal gadget columnist, had panned MobileMe. "Mossberg, our friend, is no longer writing good things about us," **Jobs said. On the spot, Jobs named a new executive to run the group.**

Simple design[256]

Mike Evangelist (yep, that's his name) still remembers one of his first meetings with Jobs. It took place in the Apple boardroom in early 2000, just a few months after Apple purchased the American division of Astarte, a German software company where Evangelist was an operations manager.

Phil Schiller, Apple's long-time head of marketing, put Evangelist on a team charged with coming up with ideas for a DVD-burning program that Apple planned to release on high-end Macs -- an app that would later become iDVD.

"We had about three weeks to prepare," Evangelist says. He and another employee went to work creating beautiful mock-ups depicting the perfect interface for the new program. On the appointed day, **Evangelist and the rest of the team gathered in the boardroom. They'd brought page after page of prototype screen shots showing the new program's various windows and menu options, along with paragraphs of documentation describing how the app would work.**

"Then Steve comes in," Evangelist recalls. "He doesn't look at any of our work. He picks up a marker and goes over to the whiteboard. He draws a rectangle. 'Here's the new application,' he says. 'It's got one window. You drag your video into the window. Then you click the button that says BURN. That's it. That's what we're going to make.' "

"We were dumbfounded," Evangelist says. This wasn't how product decisions were made at his old company. Indeed, this isn't how products are planned anywhere else in the industry.

Distortion field[257]

Most tech reporters and Apple fans know of the legendary "reality distortion field," a combination of charisma, enthusiasm and sheer showmanship that could almost hypnotize those in Jobs' presence. But who originated the term? According to Hertzfeld, it was Bud Tribble, the manager of the original Macintosh software development team.

"Well, it's Steve. Steve insists that we're shipping in early 1982, and won't accept answers to the contrary. The best way to describe the situation is a term from Star Trek. **Steve has a reality distortion field.**"

View all Photos in Gallery

"A what?"

"**A reality distortion field.** In his presence, reality is malleable. He can convince anyone of practically anything. It wears off when he's not around, but it makes it hard to have realistic schedules. And there's a couple of other things you should know about working with Steve."

Calculator Construction Set[258]

Software engineer Chris Espinosa set out to demonstrate the **QuickDraw software program by drawing a calculator with it. Jobs, naturally, wasn't happy.**

We all gathered around as Chris showed the calculator to Steve and then held his breath, waiting for **Steve's reaction. "Well, it's a start,"** Steve said, "but basically, it stinks. The background colour is too dark, some lines are the wrong thickness, and the buttons are too big." Chris told Steve he'll keep changing it, until Steve thought he got it right.**

So, for a couple of days, Chris would incorporate Steve's suggestions from the previous day, but Steve would continue to find new faults each time he was shown it. Finally, Chris got a flash of inspiration.

The next afternoon, instead of a new iteration of the calculator, Chris unveiled his new approach, which he called "the Steve Jobs Roll Your Own Calculator Construction Set". Every decision regarding graphical attributes of the calculator were parameterized by pull-down menus. You could select line thicknesses, button sizes, background patterns, etc.

Make it a Porsche[259]

The late Jef Raskin, Apple's director of publications, originally envisioned the Macintosh as essentially a lunchbox shape. Jobs debated the issue with James Ferris, Apple's director of creative services.

"We need it to have a classic look, that won't go out of style, like the Volkswagen Beetle", I heard Steve tell James.

"No, that's not right." James replied. "The lines should be voluptuous, like a Ferrari."

"Not a Ferrari, that's not right either", Steve responded, apparently excited by the car comparison. "It should be more like a Porsche!" Not so coincidentally, in those days Steve was driving a Porsche 928.

Motherboard Elegant[260]

The "PC board" or **motherboard of a personal computer is typically a purely functional device, laid out in such a way as to save space and provide adequate cooling to the components mounted upon it. "Jobs wanted more.**

Steve started critiquing the layout on a purely esthetic basis. **"That part's really pretty",** he proclaimed. "But look at the memory chips. That's ugly. The lines are too close together".

George Crow, our recently hired analog engineer, interrupted Steve. **"Who cares what the PC board looks like? The only thing that's important is how well that it works. Nobody is going to see the PC board."**

Steve responded strongly. "I'm gonna see it! I want it to be as beautiful as possible, even if it's inside the box. A great carpenter isn't going to use lousy wood for the back of a cabinet, even though nobody's going to see it."

Mr Macintosh[261]

Most people know about Clippy, the much-loathed animated paper clip that appeared in versions of Microsoft Office. But Jobs wanted Apple to have its own animated figure, too. Jobs burst into Hertzfeld's office one night.

"Mr Macintosh! We've got to have Mr Macintosh!"

"Who is Mr Macintosh?" I wondered.

"Mr Macintosh is a mysterious little man who lives inside each Macintosh. He pops up every once in a while, when you least expect it, and then winks at you and disappears again. It will be so quick that you won't be sure if you saw him or not. We'll plant references in the manuals to the legend of Mr Macintosh, and **no one will know if he's real or not.**"

Unconventional Interview[262]

Some job interviews can include off-the-wall questions, brain busters designed to pressure the candidate or demonstrate his ability to think logically under pressure. **Jobs, apparently having decided the poor interviewee was doomed to fail, decided to have a bit of fun.**

The candidate wasn't sure if he heard correctly. "What did you say?"

Steve repeated the question, changing it slightly. **"Are you a virgin?"** Burrell and I started to laugh, as the candidate became more disconcerted. He didn't know how to respond.

Steve changed the subject. "How many times have you taken LSD?"

Secret Project²⁶³

Jobs reportedly dated Joan Baez, and like all men, wanted to impress her. But who was to know that what he would show off would be the unreleased Macintosh? Apple's manager of industrial design, Jerry Manock, was aghast.

One afternoon, when the project was in its advanced stages, Steve burst through the door, unannounced, in an exuberant mood. He had two guests... Joan Baez and her sister, Mimi Farina. Steve had been to lunch with them nearby and apparently could not contain himself when Joan asked him for advice on which computer to buy for her son, Gabe. Not only did he tell them about our Macintosh-in-development but he decided to SHOW it to them too. **We sat there doubly dumfounded at the disclosure of our secret project to an outsider**... who happened to be a huge celebrity... that we actually got to meet! **Hopefully Steve had them sign a non-disclosure agreement, but I never saw it.**

This was not the last time we saw Joan Baez. Steve invited her to an Apple Macintosh Black Tie "Christmas" party one February at the St. Francis Hotel in San Francisco. I have a vivid memory of being on the dance floor with my wife, waltzing between dinner courses to the music of the San Francisco Symphony Orchestra, and bumping into Joan and Steve as they went swirling by. **Apple sure knew how to throw a party!**

Winding Path²⁶⁴

Apple just announced its first new product category since the iPad. And since Steve Jobs. Follow his life path to see how he learned to create and think like a genius.

As people around the world wondered if innovation at Apple had stopped with Steve Jobs, we want to share with you a snapshot of the genius's life.

How did Steve Jobs start? His life story is not a straight line, but more like a winding path. From his early years it's clear that Jobs had no grand plan in the beginning. His search for himself took Jobs through India, Buddhism, psychedelic use, and attempts to become an astronaut and start a computer company in the Soviet Union.

However winding his path at time, Jobs did find inspiration and creativity in himself at certain periods of his life. If there is a pattern of creativity and genius that his life can reveal, here is his timeline.

Don't Settle[265]

Steve Jobs summarized his guiding principle in life in 2005 at the commencement at Stanford in a talk titled **"How to Live Before You Die"**. **He said, you've got to find what you love. And that is as true for your work as it is for your lovers. Your work is going to fill a large part of your life, and the only way to be truly satisfied is to do what you believe is great work. And the only way to do great work is to love what you do. If you haven't found it yet, keep looking. Don't settle.** As with all matters of the heart, you'll know when you find it. And, like any great relationship, it just gets better and better as the years roll on. So keep looking. Don't settle.

One More Thing[266]

**"Sometimes life hits you in the head with a brick. Don't lose faith,"
said Steve Jobs.**

Recruiting[267]

Hiring was actually one of his most important roles at Apple. He explained his philosophy in the 1980s already: "A players hire a players," he told the Mac team. "B players hire C players. Do you get it?" **He kept this philosophy that his job was to find the best possible people, to have them hire excellent people too, throughout his life "My #1 job here at Apple is to make sure that the top 100 people are A+ players. And everything else will take care of itself.** If the top 50 people are right, it just cascades down throughout the whole organization", he told Time in 1999. **He personally oversaw the hiring of all top executives, and even some talented engineers or designers, calling them up directly to leverage his celebrity status.** Some famous examples of this are his trying to hire (or acquire) the Panic and the Dropbox teams.

Jobs carried through this vision of the 'top 100' people at Apple by an annual event which he called the 'Top 100 retreat'. He took with them the Apple employees he felt were the smartest — not always the highest-ranked, mind you — and they all left to an undisclosed location where he would present them his strategy for the coming year and the long term, and try to have their feedback on it. **The Top 100 created something of a caste at Apple:** there were the 'Top 100' — the chosen ones that Steve would take with him in the proverbial life raft if he were to start Apple over again — and there were the others.

Family man[268]

Steve Job's lifestyle changed a lot after the birth of Reed, his first child with Laurene. **He took his family very seriously, and became an affectionate father.** Until the end of his life, he would keep that same way of life: that of a hard-working CEO, but one who don't choose the celebrity circuit: "What's astonishing is how normal a family life it is. Steve just never went out socially. He was home every evening", **wrote Job's biographer Walter Isaacson. Jobs himself said: "I have a very simple life. I have my family and I have Apple and Pixar. And I don't do much else."**

Indeed, Steve Jobs apparently turned into a loving father and peaceful neighbor, the sighting of whom was commonplace to the residents of Palo Alto. However, in his official biography, Isaacson reveals that the relationships between Jobs and his children was not all that idyllic. **Although he had a special relation with his son Reed, the same apparently cannot be said of his daughters.** He often had arguments with his first daughter Lisa, his child with Chrisann Brennan; he apparently did not pay much attention to Erin, his second, quiet daughter; but he liked the strong will and temper of his youngest child, daughter Eve.

Secrecy[269]

Steve Jobs learned how important secrecy was for a technology company during the development of the Macintosh. The product was originally supposed to be out in 1982, and Steve Jobs started talking about it around that time — but the release date kept slipping and slipping, until it was finally set in 1984. By then, **Jobs had already leaked most of the revolutionary product's features to the press, and the surprise was much lessened. He learned his lesson when he started NeXT two years later.** The NeXT Cube was very late, too, but no one could tell, because no release date was ever pre-announced; and the media relayed the introduction a lot because the features of the Cube were a total surprise.

Jobs has enforced this rule as strictly as he could during his second tenure at Apple. **The company had become a leakiest in Silicon Valley,** and he made sure everyone understood this was over when he came back. **It is fair to say he instilled a culture of fear to prevent Apple employees to talk about their work, on the outside, but oftentimes also among themselves.** The secrecy from outsiders has obvious motives, such as leaving competitors in the dark, not having to apologize for a late product, and of course the huge free publicity that come from both speculation and the sensational release of new products. Every employee knows this is worth millions of dollars, and that a leak would cost them their job and severe trials. Apple actually distils false information to some of its employees to track down the source of leaks, and supposedly keeps a special teams dedicated to just that: tracking leaks. It enforces these rules as hard as it can with all their business partners such as part suppliers or developers.

A little more²⁷⁰

Steven Paul Jobs was born on February 24, 1955 in San Francisco, California. **His unwed biological parents, Joanne Schieble and Abdulfattah Jandali, put him up for adoption.** Steve was adopted by Paul and Clara Jobs, a lower-middle-class couple, who moved to the suburban city of Mountain View a couple of years later.

The Santa Clara county, south of the Bay Area, became known as Silicon Valley in the early 1950s after the sprouting of a myriad of semi-conductor companies. **As a result, young Steve Jobs grew up in a neighbourhood of engineers working on electronics and other gizmos in their garages on weekends. This shaped his interest in the field as he grew up. At age 13, he met one the most important persons in his life: 18-year-old Stephen Wozniak, an electronics wiz kid, and, like Steve, an incorrigible prankster.**

Bachelor days[271]

Steve Jobs grew up in a lower-middle class suburban neighbourhood in the 1960s. **When he was a young adult, in the early 1970s, he delved into eastern mysticism, Zen Buddhism, and hippie ideals.** Then he started Apple and became a millionaire at 23, an icon of entrepreneurialism and capitalism. It is not hard to picture how big of a shock to his values this new status must have created. In his late 20s, while he was still single, Steve Jobs was not living the life of a typical young nouveau riche.

He bought a large house in Los Gatos, not far from his parents' and Apple, which he almost didn't furnish. **He kept his peculiar food habits, staying a vegan and fasting for spa few weeks - although he sometimes allowed himself some fish and even meat once in a while.** And he worked. He worked really, really hard, and spent most of his waking hours at Apple — including weekends. He didn't have many friends a time, although he socialized quite a bit, including in New York where he purchased a luxurious apartment in the San Remo Towers.

In 1984, Jobs bought the Jacking mansion in Woodside and moved in a few months later. **His life remained pretty much the same, the mansion remaining unfurnished, apart from the kitchen where a young couple he had hired prepared him his vegan meals. Steve's long-time girlfriend, Tina Redse, whom he met during that year, hated staying at the empty house.** She kept her house in Palo Alto, which was also a refuge when she and Steve would have one of their frequent fights. Finally, in the summer of 1989, he asked her to marry him, and she declined because it would "drive her crazy".

Culture #Apple[272]

Steve Jobs was told to let 'more experienced' managers run the company in his first tenure at Apple — which led to his resignation and the John Sculley debacle. That is not to say that he had no business sense at the time: in his book about Jobs, Jay Elliot recalls how he used to "dream of the time that Apple could slash its way through to a much simpler management structure, with fewer approval levels, **fewer people needing to sign off on every decision.** He used to tell me, **'Apple should be the kind of place where anybody can walk in and share his ideas with the CEO'."** Although he could never really apply his big dreams at NeXT, which remained small, he did so at Apple after his comeback. **The first priority for Steve when he came back was simplicity: "The organization is clean and simple to understand, and very accountable. Everything just got simpler. That's been one of my mantras -- focus and simplicity", he said in 2004.** In other words, the responsibilities of every employee are very clear. For each project, and every task in that project, there will be someone accountable, a so-called DRI who will be congratulated or blamed depending on how he does.

On the executive level, Steve Jobs was very explicit that everyone's job was constantly on the line. In his book Inside Apple, Adam Lashinsky explained Steve's parable of "the VP and the janitor": **he imagines his trash not being emptied for some time. When he confronts the janitor, he is told that the keys to the locks have been changed and the janitor can't do his job anymore.**

Personal beliefs[273]

Steve Jobs didn't vote when he was young, as he professed in an interview with Playboy. After he left Apple in 1985, he caressed the idea of a career in politics, which was suggested to him by his friend and fellow Los Altos Zen Centre adept, California governor Jerry Brown. But his mentor PR man Regis McKenna explained to him it wouldn't be that easy: **Steve Jobs was risking public exposure for his private life, including its darkest sides, such as abandoning his daughter or taking LSD in college. Jobs gave up the idea and eventually founded NeXT.**

As he grew older, Jobs became a supporter of the Democratic Party. He was friendly with President Clinton, whom he entertained at his house with Hillary while in office, and he invited Al Gore to join Apple's board in 2003. Although Steve didn't donate to the Democrats in his name, his wife Laurene contributed to each campaign to the fullest amount possible for an individual.

However, Steve Jobs was not a liberal on every subject. In 2011, as his health declined severely, he still accepted to attend a dinner with President Obama on February 17. He was blunt: "You're headed for a one-term presidency," he told the president, according to Steve Jobs. "To prevent that, he said, the administration needed to be a lot more business-friendly. He described how easy it was to build a factory in China, and said that it was almost impossible to do so these days in America, largely because of regulations and unnecessary costs."

Food[274]

Yet Steve Job's strongest beliefs were not political nor religious: they concerned food and health. When he was at Reed College, he had been greatly impressed by the book Mucus less Diet Healing System by Arnold Ehret. Ehret was an early-20th century nutritionist who **professed eating nothing but fruits and starch less vegetables to protect the body from the formation of mucus, which he considered the root of all diseases.** Fasting was also recommended as a most efficient way of cleansing the body from mucus. **At age 18-19, Jobs never quit berating his friends about mucus less diets** — and he held strongly to his beliefs throughout his life, even after he was diagnosed with cancer.

After a whole year as a fruitarian, cultivating apples at a hippie commune, Jobs switched to a vegan diet, which he kept his whole life — with the exception of Japanese food. **He used to love suhi and soba, and reportedly even created the original "sashimi shoba", to be served at Apple's cafeteria. Some of his favourite restaurants included Jinshō, Cagiest and Sushi Ran.** He was also a regular at the Fraiche yoghurt cafe in Palo Alto, and the local Whole Foods where he would go pick up whole wheat bread and vegetables, often barefoot. But the Jobs also cultivated their own vegetables and fruits in the large garden that Laurene had set up. **Their meals often consisted of "just one vegetable. Lots of that one vegetable. But one.** Broccoli. In season. Simply prepared. With just the right, recently snipped, herb", as Mona Simpson recalled. **As for drinks, Steve would often profess his love of Odwalla juices, and be seen with one or more bottles of Smart Water. He never drank alcohol besides the occasional glass of wine.**

Source

1. **Jimmy Wales,** Wikipedia founder and Wikia cofounder
Link : **https://www.quora.com/profile/Jimmy-Wales**

2. **Philip Cortes,** Product Manager @ Wealthfront.
Link : https://www.quora.com/profile/Philip-Cortes

3. **Suraj Pant,** Abracadabra

Link : https://www.quora.com/profile/Suraj-Pant

4. **Rory Young,** Professional Guide and Anti-Poaching Specialist
Link : https://www.quora.com/profile/Rory-Young-1

5. **Sergey Smirnov,** NYU Engineering '17
Link : https://www.quora.com/profile/Sergey-Smirnov-2

6. **William Matthies,** Planning Consultant
Link : https://www.quora.com/profile/William-Matthies

7. **Bill Lee,** Author
Link : https://www.quora.com/profile/Bill-Lee-13

8. **Wei Yeh,** Steve Jobs is my hero.
Link : https://www.quora.com/profile/Wei-Yeh

9. **Mira Zaslove,** Quora Top Writer

Link : https://www.quora.com/profile/Mira-Zaslove

10. **Bill Sheppard,** Digital media expert and all-around technology virtuoso
Link : https://www.quora.com/profile/Bill-Sheppard

11. **Charles Bouldin**
Link : https://www.quora.com/profile/Charles-Bouldin

12. **Brandon Baum,** lawyer and rouser of rabble
Link : https://www.quora.com/profile/Brandon-Baum

13. **David Metcalfe,** Generalist.
Link : https://www.quora.com/profile/David-Metcalfe

14. **Shawn King**,Host, Your Mac Life
Link : https://www.quora.com/profile/Shawn-King

15. **Geoffrey Garth**,Inventor, Designer, Dad
Link : https://www.quora.com/profile/Geoffrey-Garth

16. **Matt Rosen**,As they pulled you out of the oxygen tent, you asked for the latest party...
Link : https://www.quora.com/profile/Matt-Rosen

17. **Michael Chang**,Intern at Apple in 2010
Link : https://www.quora.com/profile/Michael-Chang

18. **Phillip Remaker**,Problem Solver
Link : https://www.quora.com/profile/Phillip-Remaker

19. **Andrew Gerber-Duffy**,Student
Link : https://www.quora.com/profile/Andrew-Gerber-Duffy

20. **Chaitanya Pandit**,Creator of @verbsapp, founded #include tech.
Link : https://www.quora.com/profile/Chaitanya-Pandit

21. **Brian Mullin**,Manifold
Link : https://www.quora.com/profile/Brian-Mullin

22. **Mark Young**
Link : https://www.quora.com/profile/Mark-Young-5

23. **Steven White**
Link : https://www.quora.com/profile/Steven-White-9

24. **Sydney Keen**,tragically ambitious yet exceptionally underwhelming
Link : https://www.quora.com/profile/Steven-White-9

25. **Timmy Chen**
Link : https://www.quora.com/profile/Timmy-Chen

26. **Michell Smith**
Link : https://www.quora.com/profile/Michell-Smith

27. **Michael VanLandingham**
Link : https://www.quora.com/profile/Michael-VanLandingham

28. **Mark Hull**,Paranoid Android.
Link : https://www.quora.com/profile/Mark-Hull

29. **Jeff Headley**
Link : https://www.quora.com/profile/Jeff-Headley

30. **Christopher Knox,**Literary fiction writer and essayist, 20 years in the health IT industry
Link : https://www.quora.com/profile/Christopher-Knox

31. **Roy Pereira,**President and Founder @ Shiny Ads
Link : https://www.quora.com/profile/Roy-Pereira
32. **Randall Edwards**
Link : https://www.quora.com/profile/Randall-Edwards

33. **Tomas Higbey**
LInk : https://www.quora.com/profile/Tomas-Higbey

34. **Prince Srivastava, Building..**
Link : https://www.quora.com/profile/Prince-Srivastava

35. **Matt McLean,**SVP Westfield Labs
Link : https://www.quora.com/profile/Matt-McLean-2

36. **Maryam Qudus**
Link : https://www.quora.com/profile/Maryam-Qudus

37. **John G. Herndon,**Senior level consultant with broad industry experience in all areas of corpor...
Link : https://www.quora.com/profile/John-G-Herndon

38. **Anvar Alikhan**
Link : https://www.quora.com/profile/Anvar-Alikhan

39. **Moe Jamil**
Link : https://www.quora.com/profile/Moe-Jamil

40. **Andre Da Costa,**Blogger, Microsoft MVP
Link : https://www.quora.com/profile/Andre-Da-Costa

41. **Sachin Kumbhar,**Optimist & Rude
Link : https://www.quora.com/profile/Sachin-Kumbhar

42. **Aleksandra Potapova**
Link : https://www.quora.com/profile/Aleksandra-Potapova

43. **Anurag Wadehra,**Marketer, Storyteller, Filmmaker
Link : https://www.quora.com/profile/Anurag-Wadehra

44. **Mircea Goia,**12 years in technology...and counting
Link : http://www.fastcompany.com/magazine/147/node/1659056

45. **Jarin Udom,**Rails/iOS dev, founder of Robot Mode
Link : https://www.quora.com/profile/Jarin-Udom

46. **Mario Sundar,**apostle for life.
Link : https://www.quora.com/profile/Mario-Sundar

47. **Warner Leedy,**avid user and former intern
Link : https://www.quora.com/profile/Warner-Leedy

48. **Frank Denbow,**Former Apple Intern
Link : https://www.quora.com/profile/Frank-Denbow

49. **Robert Scoble,**Rackspace's Futurist, studies technology and its implementation by companies ..
Link : https://www.quora.com/profile/Robert-Scoble-1

50. **Marc Canter,**Created the first music product for the Mac - MusicWorks - in 1984.
Link : https://www.quora.com/profile/Marc-Canter

51. **Steven Wang,**Student
Link : https://www.quora.com/profile/Steven-Wang-5

52. **Justin Cone,**Apple intern, 2007
Link : **https://www.quora.com/profile/Justin-Cone**

53. **Gaston Morixe,**I guy I admire a little bit too much that could be clinically considered I am...

Link : https://www.quora.com/profile/Gaston-Morixe

54. **Gerd Moe-Behrens,**CEO CytoComp
Link : https://www.quora.com/profile/Gerd-Moe-Behrens

55. **Edward Boches,**Chief Innovation Officer, Mullen. Marketer, blogger, speaker. Board member at...
Link : https://www.quora.com/profile/Edward-Boches

56. **Subhash Medatwal**
Link : https://www.quora.com/profile/Subhash-Medatwal

57. **Cinjon Resnick,**when i was young and moving fast
Link : https://www.quora.com/profile/Cinjon-Resnick

58. **Shrey Banga**
Link : https://www.quora.com/profile/Shrey-Banga

59. **Linh Vuong Nguyen,**MIT Class of 2017, Computer Science, Traveler and Music lover
Link : https://www.quora.com/profile/Linh-Vuong-Nguyen

278

60. **Anonymous**
Link : This Stuff Doesn't Change the World': Disability and Steve Jobs' Legacy | Wired Business | Wired.com

61. **Steven Frank**
Link : https://www.quora.com/profile/Steven-Frank

62. **Josh Anon,**Product and Startup Guy
Link : https://www.quora.com/profile/Josh-Anon

63. **Jim Morris,**Professor of Computer Science at CMU in Pittsburgh
Link : https://www.quora.com/profile/Jim-Morris

64. **Chris Connors,**Lead Interaction Designer, Keynote '09, Keynote Remote, Numbers (iOS), iWork....
Link : https://www.quora.com/profile/Chris-Connors

65. **Milton Drepaul,**Educator,Writer,Editor. Lived in small places as well as large cities. Medita...
Link : https://www.quora.com/profile/Milton-Drepaul

66. **Laura Neish**
Link : https://www.quora.com/profile/Laura-Neish

67. **Anonymous**
Link : http://www.gamasutra.com/view/ne...

68. **Skip Steuart**
Link : https://www.quora.com/profile/Skip-Steuart-1

69. **Ted Matsumura**

Link : https://www.quora.com/profile/Ted-Matsumura

70. **Shubham Jain**
Link : https://www.quora.com/profile/Shubham-Jain-252

71. **Ravi Rasadiya,**HackerRanker, Googloholic,Motivator,CSE Student, Java Developer , Deep Thinker
Link : https://www.quora.com/profile/Ravi-Rasadiya

72. **Dev Bhatt**
Link : https://www.quora.com/profile/Dev-Bhatt-4

73. **Dan Zhang**,Computer Engineering PhD student at UT Austin; interned at Microsoft and Apple
Link : https://www.quora.com/profile/Dan-Zhang-1

74. **Jeff Beckham**,Writer, editor, researcher, inquisitive person
Link : https://www.quora.com/profile/Jeff-Beckham

75. **Gayatri Gajupaka**
Link : https://www.quora.com/profile/Gayatri-Gajupaka-1

76. **Vedant Shrivastava**,Apple Pundit, Software Developer, Team Manager.
Link : https://www.quora.com/profile/Vedant-Shrivastava

77. **Manish Joshi**,Maths Lover | Chess Player
Link : https://www.quora.com/profile/Manish-Joshi-63

78. **Craig Good**
Link : https://www.quora.com/profile/Craig-Good

79. **Amit Chaudhary**,Programming, Users & Peer focused, SF bay area, Adventure, Travel
Link : https://www.quora.com/profile/Amit-Chaudhary

80. **Ashlesha Sharma**,Explorer
Link : https://www.quora.com/profile/Ashlesha-Sharma-1

81. **Markus Birth**,IT Engineer at WeltN24 GmbH, Berlin, Germany
Link : https://www.quora.com/profile/Markus-Birth

82. **Pedro Gil Nieva**,Serial Entrepreneur, addicted to technology.
Link : https://www.quora.com/profile/Pedro-Gil-Nieva

83. **Jonathan Rotenberg**
Link : https://www.quora.com/profile/Jonathan-Rotenberg

84. **Luis Gerardo Silvetti**
Link : https://www.quora.com/profile/Luis-Gerardo-Silvetti

85. Jason Hirschhorn, in CNET, Feb 2011

Link : http://www.cnet.com/news/steve-jobs-once-nixed-my-music-subscription-pitch/

86. Jim Gianopulos, in Hollywood Reporter, Oct 21, 2011

Link : http://www.hollywoodreporter.com/news/jim-gianopulos-steve-jobs-dead-248311

87. **Gawker, Mar 31, 2010**

Link : http://gawker.com/5506526/a-treasure-trove-of-steve-jobs-stories

88. **Gawker, Mar 31, 2010**

Link : http://gawker.com/5506526/a-treasure-trove-of-steve-jobs-stories

89. **Time Magazine, Oct 18, 1999**

Link : http://content.time.com/time/magazine/article/0,9171,992258,00.html

90. **Reuters, Jan 1998**

Link : http://edition.cnn.com/TECH/9801/01/apple.oracle.reut/index.html

91. **Ken Segall (former Apple ad man), Dec 6, 2011**

Link : http://kensegall.com/2011/12/apples-upside-down-thinking/

92. **Steve Wozniak, interview with Dan Lyons, Oct 11, 2011**

Link : http://www.realdanlyons.com/blog/2011/10/11/a-conversation-with-woz/

93. **CNN The Marquee Blog, Dec 15, 2011**

Link : http://marquee.blogs.cnn.com/2011/12/15/diane-keaton-i-couldve-dated-steve-jobs/

94. **Bono, Rolling Stone, Oct 7, 2011**

Link : http://www.rollingstone.com/music/news/exclusive-bono-on-steve-jobs-rock-and-roll-spirit-20111007

95. **Bono, Rolling Stone, Oct 7, 2011**

Link : http://www.rollingstone.com/music/news/exclusive-bono-on-steve-jobs-rock-and-roll-spirit-20111007

96. **Cult of Mac, Oct 8, 2011**

Link : http://www.cultofmac.com/111862/i-installed-steve-jobs-trampoline-me-steve-stories/

97. Fast Company, Dec 19, 2007

Link : http://www.fastcompany.com/node/48286/print

98. Ken Segall interview, Cult of Mac, Nov 3, 2009

Link : http://www.cultofmac.com/20172/20172/

99. Newsweek, Jul 25, 2004

Link : http://www.thedailybeast.com/

100. Mac Rumors, Dec 19, 2011

Link : http://www.macrumors.com/2011/12/19/ipod-shuffle-signed-by-steve-jobs-available-on-ebay/

101. Edible Apple, Oct 20, 2011

Link : http://www.edibleapple.com/2011/10/20/john-mayer-reflects-on-steve-jobs-recounts-getting-a-pre-release-iphone/

102. Simson Garfinkel on Lotus Improv, 1991

Link : https://simson.net/clips/1991/1991.NW.Improv.html

103. Lucas Haley, FOX News, Oct 6, 2011

Link : http://www.foxnews.com/tech/2011/10/06/insanely-great-20-minutes-on-phone-with-steve-jobs.html

104. David Bunnell, Cult of Mac, May 4, 2010

Link : http://www.foxnews.com/tech/2011/10/06/insanely-great-20-minutes-on-phone-with-steve-jobs.html

105. David Bunnell, Cult of Mac, Apr 20, 2010

Link : http://www.cultofmac.com/39023/my-close-encounters-with-steve-jobs-meeting-steve/

106. **David Bunnell, Cult of Mac, Apr 23, 2010**

Link : http://www.cultofmac.com/39039/steve-jobs-tells-us-to-belly-up-to-the-bar-close-encounters-with-steve-jobs/

107. **David Bunnell, Cult of Mac, Apr 26, 2010**

Link : http://www.cultofmac.com/39080/steve-jobs-poses-for-1st-cover-of-macworld-then-changes-mind-recollections/

108. **Lisen Stromberg, Aug 29, 2011**

Link : https://lisenstromberg.wordpress.com/2011/08/29/my-neighbor-steve-jobs/

109. **Dave Winer, Sep 30, 1997**

Link : http://scripting.com/davenet/stories/beerFoodAndSteve.html

110. **The Perfect Thing by Steven Levy**

Link : https://www.amazon.com/Perfect-Thing-Shuffles-Commerce-Coolness-ebook/dp/B000MGATVC?ie=UTF8&camp=1789&creative=9325&creativeASIN=B000MGATVC&linkCode=as2&redirect=true&ref_=as_li_qf_sp_asin_il_tl&tag=allaboustevjo-20

111. **The Perfect Thing by Steven Levy**

Link : https://www.amazon.com/Perfect-Thing-Shuffles-Commerce-Coolness-ebook/dp/B000MGATVC?ie=UTF8&camp=1789&creative=9325&creativeASIN=B000MGATVC&linkCode=as2&redirect=true&ref_=as_li_qf_sp_asin_il_tl&tag=allaboustevjo-20

112. **The Perfect Thing by Steven Levy**

Link : https://www.amazon.com/Perfect-Thing-Shuffles-Commerce-Coolness-ebook/dp/B000MGATVC?ie=UTF8&camp=1789&creative=9325&creativeASIN=B000MGATVC&linkCode=as2&redirect=true&ref_=as_li_qf_sp_asin_il_tl&tag=allaboustevjo-20

113. **The Perfect Thing by Steven Levy**

Link : https://www.amazon.com/Perfect-Thing-Shuffles-Commerce-Coolness-ebook/dp/B000MGATVC?

ie=UTF8&camp=1789&creative=9325&creativeASIN=B000MGATVC&linkCode=as2&redir
ect=true&ref_=as_li_qf_sp_asin_il_tl&tag=allaboustevjo-20

114. The Perfect Thing by Steven Levy

Link : https://www.amazon.com/Perfect-Thing-Shuffles-Commerce-Coolness-
ebook/dp/B000MGATVC?
ie=UTF8&camp=1789&creative=9325&creativeASIN=B000MGATVC&linkCode=as2&redir
ect=true&ref_=as_li_qf_sp_asin_il_tl&tag=allaboustevjo-20

115. Ryan Block, gdgt, Aug 26, 2011

Link : http://www.engadget.com/discuss/share-your-steve-jobs-stories-frt/

116. Wil Shipley, @wilshipley, Twitter, Aug 27, 2011

Link : https://twitter.com/wilshipley/status/107555737575763968

117. Stephen Wolfram, Oct 6, 2011

Link : http://blog.stephenwolfram.com/2011/10/steve-jobs-a-few-memories/

118. Neven Morgan, Oct 5, 2011

Link : http://mrgan.tumblr.com/post/11090229578/steve

119. Hayashi Nobuyuki, Dec 2011

Link : http://www.nippon.com/en/currents/d00010/

120. Harvard Business School, Jun 16, 2003

Link : http://hbswk.hbs.edu/archive/3533.html

121. Huffington Post, Oct 20, 2011

Link : http://www.huffingtonpost.com/entry/steve-jobs-biography-obama_n_1022786.html?
section=india

122. Newsweek, Oct 24, 1988

Link : http://www.thedailybeast.com/

123. **Rolling Stone, Oct 7, 2011**

Link : http://www.rollingstone.com/music/news/steve-jobs-music-vision-20111007?print=true

124. **Rolling Stone, Oct 7, 2011**

Link : http://www.rollingstone.com/music/news/steve-jobs-music-vision-20111007?print=true

125. **Newsweek, May 18, 1998**

Link : http://www.thedailybeast.com/

126. **John Lilly, Oct 9, 2011**

Link : http://john.jubjubs.net/2011/10/09/steve-jobs/

127. **Steven Levy, Wired, Oct 5, 2011**

Link : http://www.wired.com/2011/10/jobs/all/1

128. **Brett Lovelady, Aug 26, 2011**

Link : http://www.fastcodesign.com/1664874/xbox-designer-on-working-next-door-to-steve-jobs

129. **Mark Parker, president and CEO of Nike**

Link : http://www.fastcompany.com/section/30-second-mba

130. **George Bodenheimer, president of ESPN, FastCompany, Oct 5, 2011**

Link : http://www.fastcompany.com/1776100/first-time-i-met-steve-jobs

131. **Fordbes, Dec 14, 2011**

Link : http://www.forbes.com/forbes/welcome/

132. **Ben Rosen, Oct 22, 2011**

Link : http://www.benrosen.com/2011/10/memories-of-steve.html

133. **Walt Mossberg, Oct 5, 2011**

Link : http://allthingsd.com/?p=129366&ak_action=printable

134. **Walt Mossberg, Oct 5, 2011**

Link : http://allthingsd.com/?p=129366&ak_action=printable

135. **Walt Mossberg, Oct 5, 2011**

Link : http://allthingsd.com/?p=129366&ak_action=printable

136. **Walt Mossberg, Oct 5, 2011**

Link : http://allthingsd.com/?p=129366&ak_action=printable

137. **Cabel Sasser, The Audion Story, 2007**

Link : http://www.panic.com/extras/audionstory/

138. **Cabel Sasser, The Audion Story, 2007**

Link : http://www.panic.com/extras/audionstory/

139. **Joe Eaton and Ron Sullivan, SF Chronicle, Feb 2012**

Link : http://www.sfgate.com/homeandgarden/thedirt/article/Steve-Jobs-gardener-describes-mutual-appreciation-3356392.php

140. **Dag Kittlaus, co-founder of Siri, about Apple's 2010 acquisition**

Link : http://www.networkworld.com/article/2221246/smartphones/steve-jobs-wasn-t-a-fan-of-the-siri-name.html

141. **Ken Segall on the name 'iMac'**

Link : http://bits.blogs.nytimes.com/2012/07/06/ken-segall-insanely-simple/?pagewanted=all&_r=0

142. **Ken Segall on the name 'NeXT'**

Link : http://bits.blogs.nytimes.com/2012/07/06/ken-segall-insanely-simple/?pagewanted=all

286

143. **Matthew Panzarino, The Next Web, October 2012**

Link : http://thenextweb.com/apple/2012/10/04/the-story-of-a-lost-time-capsule-containing-steve-jobs-lisa-mouse/

144. **The 'new' Jobs shows two faces, The San Jose Mercury News, August 10, 1997**

Link :
http://web.archive.org/web/19971018080221/http://www.sjmercury.com/business/apple/jobs08
0997.htm

145. **The 'new' Jobs shows two faces, The San Jose Mercury News, August 10, 1997**

Link :
http://web.archive.org/web/19971018080221/http://www.sjmercury.com/business/apple/jobs08
0997.htm

146. **Randy Adams to Forbes, Oct 3 2012**

Link : http://www.forbes.com/sites/connieguglielmo/2012/10/03/untold-stories-about-steve-jobs-friends-and-colleagues-share-their-memories/#76d462af28a6

147. **Randy Adams to Forbes, Oct 3 2012**

Link : http://www.forbes.com/sites/connieguglielmo/2012/10/03/untold-stories-about-steve-jobs-friends-and-colleagues-share-their-memories/#fc57eae28a6b

148. **Marc Andreessen to Forbes, Oct 3 2012**

Link : http://www.forbes.com/sites/connieguglielmo/2012/10/03/untold-stories-about-steve-jobs-friends-and-colleagues-share-their-memories/#72a6cab528a6

149. **Nolan Bushnell to Forbes, Oct 3 2012**

Link : http://www.forbes.com/sites/connieguglielmo/2012/10/03/untold-stories-about-steve-jobs-friends-and-colleagues-share-their-memories/#7bd7eddd28a6

150. **Regis McKenna to Forbes, Oct 3 2012**

Link : http://www.forbes.com/sites/connieguglielmo/2012/10/03/untold-stories-about-steve-jobs-friends-and-colleagues-share-their-memories/

151. **Business Insider, July 27 2012**

Link : http://www.businessinsider.com/how-steve-jobs-almost-leaked-the-original-iphones-existence-2012-7?IR=T

152. **Suzanne, Oct 7 2011**

Link : https://walkingpapers.wordpress.com/2011/10/07/lunch-with-steve-jobs/

153. **Wired, Jan 18 2008**

Link : http://www.wired.com/2008/01/celebrity-bitch/

154. **Inspirational Story**

Link : http://dyslexiahelp.umich.edu/success-stories/steve-jobs

155. **Steve Jobs Secretive Private Life**

Link : http://abcnews.go.com/Technology/steve-jobs-secret-private-life/story?id=14678496

156. Ex dishes on sex life with Steve Jobs
Link : http://nypost.com/2013/10/15/steve-jobs-ex-reveals-their-explosive-relationship/

157. **Early life and childhood**
Link : https://www.yahoo.com/news/blogs/technology-blog/8-things-didn-t-know-life-steve-jobs-172130955.html

158. **College dropout**

Link : https://www.yahoo.com/news/blogs/technology-blog/8-things-didn-t-know-life-steve-jobs-172130955.html

159. **Fibbed to his Apple co-founder about a job at Atari**

Link : https://www.yahoo.com/news/blogs/technology-blog/8-things-didn-t-know-life-steve-jobs-172130955.html

160. **The wife he leaves behind**
Link : https://www.yahoo.com/news/blogs/technology-blog/8-things-didn-t-know-life-steve-jobs-172130955.html

161. His sister is a famous author

Link : https://www.yahoo.com/news/blogs/technology-blog/8-things-didn-t-know-life-steve-jobs-172130955.html

162. Celebrity romances

Link : https://www.yahoo.com/news/blogs/technology-blog/8-things-didn-t-know-life-steve-jobs-172130955.html

163. His first daughter

Link : https://www.yahoo.com/news/blogs/technology-blog/8-things-didn-t-know-life-steve-jobs-172130955.html

164. Alternative lifestyle

Link : https://www.yahoo.com/news/blogs/technology-blog/8-things-didn-t-know-life-steve-jobs-172130955.html

165. His fortune

Link : https://www.yahoo.com/news/blogs/technology-blog/8-things-didn-t-know-life-steve-jobs-172130955.html

166. Apple (Source: Flickr/pj_vanf)

Link : http://www.boomsbeat.com/articles/13/20131231/50-facts-that-you-didnt-know-about-steve-jobs.htm

167. Apple (Source: Flickr/pj_vanf)

Link : http://www.boomsbeat.com/articles/13/20131231/50-facts-that-you-didnt-know-about-steve-jobs.htm

168. Apple (Source: Flickr/pj_vanf)

Link : http://www.boomsbeat.com/articles/13/20131231/50-facts-that-you-didnt-know-about-steve-jobs.htm

169. **Apple (Source: Flickr/pj_vanf)**

Link : http://www.boomsbeat.com/articles/13/20131231/50-facts-that-you-didnt-know-about-steve-jobs.htm

170. **Apple (Source: Flickr/pj_vanf)**

Link : http://www.boomsbeat.com/articles/13/20131231/50-facts-that-you-didnt-know-about-steve-jobs.htm

171. **Apple (Source: Flickr/pj_vanf)**

Link : http://www.boomsbeat.com/articles/13/20131231/50-facts-that-you-didnt-know-about-steve-jobs.htm

172. **Apple (Source: Flickr/pj_vanf)**

Link : http://www.boomsbeat.com/articles/13/20131231/50-facts-that-you-didnt-know-about-steve-jobs.htm

173. **Apple (Source: Flickr/pj_vanf)**

Link : http://www.boomsbeat.com/articles/13/20131231/50-facts-that-you-didnt-know-about-steve-jobs.htm

174. **Apple (Source: Flickr/pj_vanf)**

Link : http://www.boomsbeat.com/articles/13/20131231/50-facts-that-you-didnt-know-about-steve-jobs.htm

175. **Apple (Source: Flickr/pj_vanf)**

Link : http://www.boomsbeat.com/articles/13/20131231/50-facts-that-you-didnt-know-about-steve-jobs.htm

176. **Apple (Source: Flickr/pj_vanf)**

Link : http://www.boomsbeat.com/articles/13/20131231/50-facts-that-you-didnt-know-about-steve-jobs.htm

177. **Apple (Source: Flickr/pj_vanf)**

Link : http://www.boomsbeat.com/articles/13/20131231/50-facts-that-you-didnt-know-about-steve-jobs.htm

178. **Apple (Source: Flickr/pj_vanf)**

Link : http://www.boomsbeat.com/articles/13/20131231/50-facts-that-you-didnt-know-about-steve-jobs.htm

179. **Apple (Source: Flickr/pj_vanf)**

Link : http://www.boomsbeat.com/articles/13/20131231/50-facts-that-you-didnt-know-about-steve-jobs.htm

180. **Apple (Source: Flickr/pj_vanf)**

Link : http://www.boomsbeat.com/articles/13/20131231/50-facts-that-you-didnt-know-about-steve-jobs.htm

181. **Apple (Source: Flickr/pj_vanf)**

Link : http://www.boomsbeat.com/articles/13/20131231/50-facts-that-you-didnt-know-about-steve-jobs.htm

182. **Apple (Source: Flickr/pj_vanf)**

Link : http://www.boomsbeat.com/articles/13/20131231/50-facts-that-you-didnt-know-about-steve-jobs.htm

183. **Apple (Source: Flickr/pj_vanf)**

Link : http://www.boomsbeat.com/articles/13/20131231/50-facts-that-you-didnt-know-about-steve-jobs.htm

184. **Apple (Source: Flickr/pj_vanf)**

Link : http://www.boomsbeat.com/articles/13/20131231/50-facts-that-you-didnt-know-about-steve-jobs.htm

185. **Apple (Source: Flickr/pj_vanf)**

Link : http://www.boomsbeat.com/articles/13/20131231/50-facts-that-you-didnt-know-about-steve-jobs.htm

186. **Apple (Source: Flickr/pj_vanf)**

Link : http://www.boomsbeat.com/articles/13/20131231/50-facts-that-you-didnt-know-about-steve-jobs.htm

187. **Apple (Source: Flickr/pj_vanf)**

Link : http://www.boomsbeat.com/articles/13/20131231/50-facts-that-you-didnt-know-about-steve-jobs.htm

188. **Apple (Source: Flickr/pj_vanf)**

Link : http://www.boomsbeat.com/articles/13/20131231/50-facts-that-you-didnt-know-about-steve-jobs.htm

189. **Apple (Source: Flickr/pj_vanf)**

Link : http://www.boomsbeat.com/articles/13/20131231/50-facts-that-you-didnt-know-about-steve-jobs.htm

190. Apple (Source: Flickr/pj_vanf)

Link : http://www.boomsbeat.com/articles/13/20131231/50-facts-that-you-didnt-know-about-steve-jobs.htm

191. Apple (Source: Flickr/pj_vanf)

Link : http://www.boomsbeat.com/articles/13/20131231/50-facts-that-you-didnt-know-about-steve-jobs.htm

192. Apple (Source: Flickr/pj_vanf)

Link : http://www.boomsbeat.com/articles/13/20131231/50-facts-that-you-didnt-know-about-steve-jobs.htm

193. Apple (Source: Flickr/pj_vanf)

Link : http://www.boomsbeat.com/articles/13/20131231/50-facts-that-you-didnt-know-about-steve-jobs.htm

194. **How Steve Jobs Behaves in Public**

Link : http://gawker.com/5506526/a-treasure-trove-of-steve-jobs-stories

195. **Was the Steve Jobs and Eric Schmidt Meeting a Publicity Stunt? Probably Not**

Link :http://gawker.com/5506526/a-treasure-trove-of-steve-jobs-stories

196. **BootHillBossanova's comment**

Link : http://gawker.com/5506526/a-treasure-trove-of-steve-jobs-stories

197. <u>**steve.krupf's comment**</u>:

Link : http://gawker.com/5506526/a-treasure-trove-of-steve-jobs-stories

198. **The Sloppy CEO: A brush with a potential tantrum**

Link : http://gawker.com/5506526/a-treasure-trove-of-steve-jobs-stories

199. **Stopping to chat up a fellow cancer patient**

Link : http://gawker.com/5506526/a-treasure-trove-of-steve-jobs-stories

200. **Steve Jobs waits in line for food like a normal person**

Link : http://gawker.com/5506526/a-treasure-trove-of-steve-jobs-stories

201. **Steve Jobs does not wait in line for food like some peon**

Link : http://gawker.com/5506526/a-treasure-trove-of-steve-jobs-stories

202. **Do You Know Who I Am?**
Link : http://gawker.com/5506526/a-treasure-trove-of-steve-jobs-stories

203. **Steve Jobs *does* shake hands with strangers, and remembers names as well as a politician**

Link : http://gawker.com/5506526/a-treasure-trove-of-steve-jobs-stories

204. **He's good with kids and apparent crazy people**

Link : http://gawker.com/5506526/a-treasure-trove-of-steve-jobs-stories

205. He takes care of his vehicle

Link : http://gawker.com/5506526/a-treasure-trove-of-steve-jobs-stories

206. How Steve Jobs Used Masterful Storytelling to Motivate Employees

Link : http://www.inc.com/graham-winfrey/4-ways-steve-jobs-used-storytelling-to-inspire-apple-workers.html

207. The ceremony

Link : http://www.inc.com/graham-winfrey/4-ways-steve-jobs-used-storytelling-to-inspire-apple-workers.html

208. Admit you don't have all the answers.

Link : http://www.inc.com/graham-winfrey/4-ways-steve-jobs-used-storytelling-to-inspire-apple-workers.html

209. Tap into your audience's FOMO.

Link : http://www.inc.com/graham-winfrey/4-ways-steve-jobs-used-storytelling-to-inspire-apple-workers.html

210. Do more listening than talking.

Link : http://www.inc.com/graham-winfrey/4-ways-steve-jobs-used-storytelling-to-inspire-apple-workers.html

211. He was a responsible parent

Link : http://www.computerworld.com/article/2682611/7-steve-jobs-stories-we-learned-this-month.html

212. His office remains

Link : http://www.computerworld.com/article/2682611/7-steve-jobs-stories-we-learned-this-month.html

213. His words are in your Mac

Link : http://www.computerworld.com/article/2682611/7-steve-jobs-stories-we-learned-this-month.html

214. He was a teacher

Link : http://www.computerworld.com/article/2682611/7-steve-jobs-stories-we-learned-this-month.html

215. He was amazed by Xerox

Link : http://www.computerworld.com/article/2682611/7-steve-jobs-stories-we-learned-this-month.html

216. He needed to be convinced to run Apple again

Link : http://www.computerworld.com/article/2682611/7-steve-jobs-stories-we-learned-this-month.html

217. The Apple watch

Link : http://www.computerworld.com/article/2682611/7-steve-jobs-stories-we-learned-this-month.html

218. "The Second Coming of Steven Jobs"

Link : http://www.esquire.com/news-politics/a11185/second-coming-of-steve-jobs-1286/

219. "Steve Jobs and the Portal to the Invisible"

Link : http://www.esquire.com/news-politics/a4955/steve-jobs-1008/

220. Allen Paltrow, Oct 6, 2011

Link : http://allaboutstevejobs.com/sayings/stevejobsanecdotes_all.php

221. Fortune, Jul 31, 2000

Link : http://allaboutstevejobs.com/sayings/stevejobsanecdotes_all.php

222. The New York Times, Jan 18, 1997

Link : http://allaboutstevejobs.com/sayings/stevejobsanecdotes_all.php

223. Eric Schmidt, Business Week, Oct 6, 2011

Link : http://allaboutstevejobs.com/sayings/stevejobsanecdotes_all.php

224. Interview of Michael Scott, Business Insider, May 24, 2011

Link : http://allaboutstevejobs.com/sayings/stevejobsanecdotes_all.php

225. Interview of Michael Scott, Business Insider, May 24, 2011

Link : http://allaboutstevejobs.com/sayings/stevejobsanecdotes_all.php

226. Interview of Michael Scott, Business Insider, May 24, 2011

Link : http://allaboutstevejobs.com/sayings/stevejobsanecdotes_all.php

227. Fortune, Aug 25, 2011

Link : http://allaboutstevejobs.com/sayings/stevejobsanecdotes_all.php

228. David A. Kaplan, Fortune, Oct 11, 2011

Link : http://allaboutstevejobs.com/sayings/stevejobsanecdotes_all.php

229. **David A. Kaplan, Fortune, Oct 11, 2011**

Link : http://allaboutstevejobs.com/sayings/stevejobsanecdotes_all.php

230. **David A. Kaplan, Fortune, Oct 11, 2011**

Link : http://allaboutstevejobs.com/sayings/stevejobsanecdotes_all.php

231. **Walter Isaacson interview, Fortune, Dec 27, 2011**

Link : http://allaboutstevejobs.com/sayings/stevejobsanecdotes_all.php

232. **Walter Isaacson interview, Fortune, Dec 27, 2011**

Link : http://allaboutstevejobs.com/sayings/stevejobsanecdotes_all.php

233. **Walter Isaacson interview, Fortune, Dec 27, 2011**

Link : http://allaboutstevejobs.com/sayings/stevejobsanecdotes_all.php

234. **John Sculley interview, Business Week, Oct 6, 2011**

Link : http://allaboutstevejobs.com/sayings/stevejobsanecdotes_all.php

235. **Wired, Oct 2011**

Link : http://allaboutstevejobs.com/sayings/stevejobsanecdotes_all.php

236. **David Chao, Fortune, Oct 6, 2011**

Link : http://allaboutstevejobs.com/sayings/stevejobsanecdotes_all.php

237. **Noah Wyle, Fortune, Oct 7, 2011**

Link : http://allaboutstevejobs.com/sayings/stevejobsanecdotes_all.php

238. **Playboy, Feb 1985**

Link : http://allaboutstevejobs.com/sayings/stevejobsanecdotes_all.php

239. **Stephen Fry, Oct 6, 2011**

Link : http://allaboutstevejobs.com/sayings/stevejobsanecdotes_all.php

240. **Business Week, Jan 26, 2006**

Link : http://allaboutstevejobs.com/sayings/stevejobsanecdotes_all.php

241. **Business Week, Oct 24, 1988**

Link : http://allaboutstevejobs.com/sayings/stevejobsanecdotes_all.php

242. **Business Week, Oct 24, 1988**

Link : http://allaboutstevejobs.com/sayings/stevejobsanecdotes_all.php

243. **Business Week, Oct 6, 2011**

Link : http://allaboutstevejobs.com/sayings/stevejobsanecdotes_all.php

244. **Business Week, Oct 6, 2011**

Link : http://allaboutstevejobs.com/sayings/stevejobsanecdotes_all.php

245. **Business Week, Oct 6, 2011**

Link : http://allaboutstevejobs.com/sayings/stevejobsanecdotes_all.php

246. **Business Week, Oct 6, 2011**

Link : http://allaboutstevejobs.com/sayings/stevejobsanecdotes_all.php

247. **Steve Jurvetson on Steve Jobs, Business Week, Oct 6, 2011**

Link : http://allaboutstevejobs.com/sayings/stevejobsanecdotes_all.php

248. **Steve Jurvetson on Steve Jobs, Business Week, Oct 6, 2011**

Link : http://allaboutstevejobs.com/sayings/stevejobsanecdotes_all.php

249. **Henry Nicholas, Business Week, Oct 6, 2011**

Link : http://allaboutstevejobs.com/sayings/stevejobsanecdotes_all.php

250. **Matt Drance, Business Week, Oct 6, 2011**

Link : http://allaboutstevejobs.com/sayings/stevejobsanecdotes_all.php

251. **Business Week, Oct 12, 2011**

Link : http://allaboutstevejobs.com/sayings/stevejobsanecdotes_all.php

252. **Business Week, Oct 12, 2011**

Link : http://allaboutstevejobs.com/sayings/stevejobsanecdotes_all.php

253. **MacWorld, Aug 9 2007**

Link : http://allaboutstevejobs.com/sayings/stevejobsanecdotes_all.php

254. **Steve Jobs on the original iPod**
Link : **http://dandemeyere.com/blog/5-most-inspiring-steve-jobs-stories**

255. **Steve Jobs on dealing with a failed product**
Link : **http://dandemeyere.com/blog/5-most-inspiring-steve-jobs-stories**

256. Steve Jobs on simple design

Link : http://dandemeyere.com/blog/5-most-inspiring-steve-jobs-stories

257. Jobs and the "Reality Distortion Field"

Link : http://in.pcmag.com/mac-desktops/93127/news/the-best-steve-jobs-stories-the-macintosh-years

258. The Steve Jobs Roll Your Own Calculator Construction Set
Link : http://in.pcmag.com/mac-desktops/93127/news/the-best-steve-jobs-stories-the-macintosh-years

259. The Mac: Make it a Porsche!

Link : http://in.pcmag.com/mac-desktops/93127/news/the-best-steve-jobs-stories-the-macintosh-years

260. Even the Motherboard Must Be Elegant

Link : http://in.pcmag.com/mac-desktops/93127/news/the-best-steve-jobs-stories-the-macintosh-years

261. Meet Mister Macintosh
Link : http://in.pcmag.com/mac-desktops/93127/news/the-best-steve-jobs-stories-the-macintosh-years

262. An Unconventional Interview

Link : http://in.pcmag.com/mac-desktops/93127/news/the-best-steve-jobs-stories-the-macintosh-years

263. Here Joan, See Our Secret Project
Link : http://in.pcmag.com/mac-desktops/93127/news/the-best-steve-jobs-stories-the-macintosh-years

264. **The Winding Path**

Link : http://fundersandfounders.com/how-steve-jobs-started/

265. **Keep Looking, Don't Settle**
Link : http://fundersandfounders.com/how-steve-jobs-started/

266. **And One More Thing**
Link : http://fundersandfounders.com/how-steve-jobs-started/

267. Steve Jobs and Recruiting

Link : https://www.facebook.com/SteveJobs.WalterIsaacson/

268. Steve Jobs the family man

Link : https://www.facebook.com/SteveJobs.WalterIsaacson/

269. Steve Jobs on Secrecy

Link : https://www.facebook.com/SteveJobs.WalterIsaacson/

270. A little bit about Steve....

Link : https://www.facebook.com/SteveJobs.WalterIsaacson/

271. Steve Jobs - Bachelor days

Link : https://www.facebook.com/SteveJobs.WalterIsaacson/

272. The culture Steve Jobs imposed upon #Apple

Link : https://www.facebook.com/SteveJobs.WalterIsaacson/

273. Steve Job's personal beliefs

Link : https://www.facebook.com/SteveJobs.WalterIsaacson/

274. Steve Jobs and food

Link : https://www.facebook.com/SteveJobs.WalterIsaacson/